Übungsbuch zum Schulbuch

Passend für
- **Diesterweg Camden Town 3**
- **Cornelsen English G 21 A3**
- **Cornelsen English G access 3**
- **Klett Green Line 3** (Ausgabe 2007)
- **Klett Green Line 3** (Ausgabe 2016)

Englisch 3

Gymnasium
7. Klasse

Sarah Nowotny

PONS GmbH
Stuttgart

PONS

Übungsbuch zum Schulbuch
ENGLISCH 3
Gymnasium 7. Klasse

von
Sarah Nowotny

Die Audiodateien zu diesem Titel findest du unter
www.pons.de/übungsbuch-zum-schulbuch-englisch3
oder scanne den QR-Code.

Tonstudio: Bauer Studios GmbH, Ludwigsburg
Sprecher: Samira Aziz-Kloiber, Gillian Bathmaker, Nicholas Cole, Helen Smyth, Marie-Louise Vollmer

Auflage A1 5 4 3 2 1 / 2020 2019 2018 2017

Redaktion: PONS Lernhilfen
Logoentwurf: Erwin Poell, Heidelberg
Logoüberarbeitung: Sabine Redling, Heidelberg
Umschlagfoto: Thinkstock, München (GeorgeRudy)
Einbandgestaltung: Sabine Kaufmann, Stuttgart
Satz: DTP-studio Andrea Eckhardt, Göppingen
Druck und Bindung: Gebr. Geiselberger GmbH, Altötting

Printed in Germany
ISBN 978-3-12-562530-3

Vorwort: Alles ganz einfach – the easy way!

In diesem Übungsbuch findest du:

Grammatik

Alle Grammatikthemen deiner Klasse findest du schnell, wenn du im Inhaltsverzeichnis ab Seite 4 suchst. Schlage die angegebene Seite dieses Übungsbuches auf – du findest hier viele Übungen mit unterschiedlichem Schwierigkeitsgrad. Auf den Seiten gleich nach den Übungen stehen die Lösungen.

Textverständnis

Im zweiten Buchteil findest du Übungen zu Themen, die in deiner Klassenstufe behandelt werden. Es gibt Übungen zum

- Hörverstehen
- Schreiben von eigenen Texten
- Leseverstehen
- Sprachmittlung (Mediation)

Passend zum

Schulbuch

Dieses Übungsbuch passt genau zu deinem Schulbuch. Suche dein eigenes Schulbuch auf den Seiten unseres Wegweisers – du kannst diese Seiten mit einem „Eselsohr“ oder einem Lesezeichen markieren, um sie immer schnell wieder zu finden.
Dein ganz persönlicher Wegweiser zeigt dir immer genau an, auf welcher Seite dieses Übungsbuches du findest, was bei dir in der Schule gerade dran ist. Du findest jede Unit, alle Grammatikthemen, Wortschatzübungen und alle Themen, die ihr in der Schule behandelt. So kannst du alles wiederholen und bist immer gut vorbereitet.

WEGWEISER
Passend für

- Diesterweg Camden Town 3 S. 10
- Cornelsen English G 21 A3 S. 13
- Cornelsen English G access 3 S. 17
- Klett Green Line 3 (Ausgabe 2007) S. 20
- Klett Green Line 3 (Ausgabe 2016) S. 25

Inhaltsverzeichnis

Vorwort: Alles ganz einfach – *the easy way*! 3

Inhaltsverzeichnis 4

Wegweiser zu deinem Schulbuch

Diesterweg Camden Town 3 10
Cornelsen English G21 A3 13
Cornelsen English G access 3 17
Klett Green Line 3 (Ausgabe 2007) 20
Klett Green Line 3 (Ausgabe 2016) 25

Grammatik

Zeitformen der Zukunft (*The future tenses*)

1 Das Futur mit *going to* (*The going to-future*) — She is going to miss the train. 30
2 Das Futur mit *will* (*The will-future*) — I'm sure you will like it. 31
3 Das *present progressive* mit futurischer Bedeutung (*The present progressive with future meaning*) — We're having a party on Saturday. 32
4 Das *simple present* mit futurischer Bedeutung (*The simple present with future meaning*) — The bus leaves at 10.30. 34
5 Das Futur mit *will* für spontane Entschlüsse (*The will-future for spontaneous decisions*) — I will help you carry those boxes. 35
6 Das Futur II (*The future perfect*) — She will have sent the e-mail by 5 o'clock. 36
7 Gemischte Aufgaben (*Mixed forms*) 37
→ Lösungen 40

Zeitformen der Vergangenheit (*The past tenses*)

1 Die einfache Vergangenheit (*The simple past*) — She went swimming in the sea. 43
2 Das *present perfect* (*The present perfect*) — Paul has never been to France. 45
3 Das *simple past* und das *present perfect* im Vergleich (*The simple past and the present perfect in contrast*) — Where did you go yesterday? / Have you done your homework yet? 47
4 Das *present perfect* mit *since* und *for* (*The present perfect with since and for*) — She's lived here since 2014. / I haven't seen her for months. 49
5 Die Verlaufsform des *present perfect* (*The present perfect progressive*) — It has been snowing all afternoon. 50

Inhaltsverzeichnis

6 Das Plusquamperfekt
(*The past perfect*)
Pat had lost his key, so he couldn't open the door. 52

7 Das *past progressive*
(*The past progressive*)
She wasn't watching TV. She was doing her homework. 54

8 Das *simple past* und das *past progressive*
(*The simple past and the past progressive*)
I was feeling hot, so I took off my jacket. 55

→ Lösungen 57

Bedingungssätze (*Conditional clauses*)

1 Bedingungssätze Typ 1
(*Conditional clauses, Type 1*)
I'll come with you this evening if I have time. 61

2 Bedingungssätze Typ 2
(*Conditional clauses, Type 2*)
Tom would go out with Ella if she asked him. 63

3 Bedingungssätze Typ 3
(*Conditional clauses, Type 3*)
You would have known the answer if you had listened. 66

4 Bedingungssätze – Gemischte Aufgaben
(*Conditional clauses – Mixed forms*) 69

→ Lösungen 72

Reflexivpronomen (*Reflexive pronouns*)

1 Reflexiver Gebrauch
(*Reflexive use*) myself, yourself, himself ... 75

2 Verstärkender Gebrauch I can do it myself. 77

3 *Each other* They looked at each other. 79

4 Gemischte Aufgaben (*Mixed forms*) 81

→ Lösungen 83

Modalverben und ihre Ersatzverben
(*Modals and their substitutes*)

1 Können:
can – (to) be able to 86

2 Dürfen, nicht dürfen:
can – may – mustn't – (to) be allowed to 88

3 Müssen (nicht brauchen):
must – (to) have to – needn't 90

4 Gemischte Aufgaben (*Mixed forms*) 92

→ Lösungen 94

Inhaltsverzeichnis

Besondere Formen des Adjektivs
(*Special forms of adjectives*)
1 Das Adjektiv als Nomen (*Adjectives as nouns*) — The rich often have expensive cars. 97
2 Adjektive nach bestimmten Verben (*Adjectives after certain verbs*) — to feel bad, to be hungry 99
→ Lösungen 102

Der bestimmte und der unbestimmte Artikel
(*The definite and indefinite article*)
1 Der bestimmte Artikel (*The definite article*) — the music, listen to music 104
2 Der unbestimmte Artikel (*The indefinite article*) — to have a headache 105
→ Lösungen 106

Paarwörter (*Pair words*)
1 Paarwörter (*Pair words*) — glasses, trousers, ... 107
→ Lösungen 108

Die indirekte Rede
(*Indirect speech*)
1 Direkte und indirekte Rede (*Direct and indirect speech*) — She says that she's got a new friend. 109
2 Veränderungen der Zeitform (*Tense change*) — They said that they were hungry. 111
3 Die indirekte Rede mit Einführungssatz im Präsens (*Indirect speech with reporting verb in the present*) — Nina says she will call us later. 114
4 Fragen in der indirekten Rede (*Indirect questions*) — She wanted to know where I lived. 115
5 Veränderungen der Pronomen (*Pronouns changes*) — I asked her where she was going. 117
6 Zeitangaben in der indirekten Rede (*Time expressions in indirect speech*) — that day, the year before, ... 118
7 Indirekte Aufforderungssätze (*Indirect commands*) — They warned us not to go. 120
→ Lösungen 121

Relativsätze (*Relative clauses*)
1 Relativpronomen (*Relative pronouns*) who, that, which 124
2 Notwendige Relativsätze (*Defining relative sentences*) the dog that always barks 125
3 Präpositionen im notwendigen Relativsatz (*Prepositions in defining relative clauses*) She's talking to the girl who won the prize. 127
4 Relativsätze ohne Relativpronomen (*Contact clauses*) The story she told me was true. 128
5 Gemischte Aufgaben (*Mixed forms*) 130
→ Lösungen 132

Das Passiv (*The passive*)
1 Aktiv und Passiv (*Active and passive*) 135
2 Das Passiv: Form und Gebrauch (*The passive: form and use*) 137
3 Das Passiv bei Verben mit zwei Objekten (*Passive sentences with two objects*) A film was shown to us. 139
4 Passivsätze mit *by* ... (*Passive sentences with by ...*) This song was written by him. 140
5 Gemischte Aufgaben (*Mixed forms*) 142
→ Lösungen 144

Textverständnis

In der Stadt (*Towns and cities*)

1 Wortschatz: Verkehr und Verkehrsmittel (*Vocabulary: Traffic and transport*) 148
2 Eine Anzeige am Bahnhof verstehen (*Understanding station announcements*) 151
3 Sehenswürdigkeiten (*Sightseeing and attractions*) 152
4 Wegbeschreibungen (*Asking for and understanding directions*) 155
→ Lösungen 157

Großbritannien: Geschichte und Traditionen (*Great Britain: History and traditions*)

1 Schottische Traditionen (*Scottish traditions*) 161
2 Das Leben in Wales (*Life in Wales*) 163
3 Britische Geschichte (*British history*) 165
4 Eine zeitübergreifende Geschichte schreiben (*Using the past perfect in a story*) 167
→ Lösungen 168

Sport (*Sport*)

1 Wortschatz: Sport (*Vocabulary: Sport*) 171
2 Internationale Sportsveranstaltungen (*International sporting events*) 173
3 Ein Unfallbericht (*Writing an accident report*) 175
→ Lösungen 177

Die Medien (*The media*)

1 Wortschatz: Elektronische Medien (*Vocabulary: Electronic media*) 179
2 Was ist das für ein Buch? (*What kind of book is it?*) 182
3 Zeitschriften für Teenager (*Teen magazines*) 184
4 Nachrichten verstehen: ein Radiobericht (*Understanding a radio report*) 186
5 Einen Zeitungsartikel schreiben (*Writing a newspaper article*) 188
6 Werbung (*Advertising*) 189
→ Lösungen 190

Reisen (*Travelling*)

1 Wortschatz: Bei einer Gastfamilie (*Vocabulary: Staying with a host family*) 193
2 Grenzen überqueren: verschiedene Akzente (*Crossing borders: different accents*) 196
3 Ratschläge für eine Reise (*Advice for a trip*) 197
4 Weltreise: Interkulturelle Begegnungen (*Travelling the world: discovering other cultures*) 200
5 Über eine fiktive Reise schreiben (*Imagining a future trip*) 202
→ Lösungen 203

Auf dem Land (*In the country*)

1 Die Natur (*The natural world*) 206
2 Die Tierwelt (*Wildlife*) 208
3 Land und Stadt (*Town and country*) 211
→ Lösungen 212

Musik und Unterhaltung (*Music and entertainment*)

1 Musik (*Music*) 215
2 Probleme in der Familie, Kompromisse (*Problems with your family, compromises*) 217
3 Ein Interview führen (*Interviewing someone*) 219
→ Lösungen 222

Das Leben als Teenager (*Teenage life*)

1 Gefühle ausdrücken (*Talking about your feelings*) 226
2 Umzug in ein anderes Land (*Moving to a different country*) 228
3 Etwas aus einer anderen Perspektive erzählen (*Telling a story from a different point of view*) 232
→ Lösungen 234

Liste der unregelmäßigen Verben (*List of irregular verbs*) 236 – 238

Unit 1 – Camden Town 3

Grammatik

- **R: Die Zeitformen des Verbs** (Tenses) Seite 30 – 60

Wortschatz – Textverständnis

Leaving home Seite 228

Personal problems Seite 226

Telling a story from a different point of view Seite 232

Unit 2 – Camden Town 3

Grammatik

- **Bedingungssätze, Typ 1** (Conditional clauses, type 1) Seite 61
  We will play inside if it rains.
- **Bedingungssätze, Typ 2** (Conditional clauses, type 2) Seite 63
  If he didn't eat the soup, his mother would be angry.
- **Notwendige Relativsätze** (Defining relative clauses) Seite 125
  The girl who lives next door … / The book that I read is about dogs.
- **Relativsätze ohne Relativpronomen** (Contact clauses) Seite 128
  The boy I met last year … / The book I like best …

Wortschatz – Textverständnis

Wales Seite 163

School life Seite 217

Unit 3 – Camden Town 3

Grammatik

- **Das Plusquamperfekt** (The past perfect) Seite 52
  He had seen her before.
- **Der bestimmte und der unbestimmte Artikel** (The definite and the indefinite article) Seite 104
  Dinner is ready. / The food is on the table.
- **Das Passiv** (The passive) Seite 135
  The stolen money has been found.

Wortschatz – Textverständnis

Science fiction Seite 202

British history Seite 165

Unit 4 – Camden Town 3

Grammatik

- **Indirekte Rede** (Reported speech) Seite 109
  She says that he is not her boyfriend.
- **Reflexivpronomen** (Reflexive pronouns) Seite 75
  myself, yourself, …
- **Das reziproke Pronomen *each other*** (The reciprocal pronoun *each other*) Seite 79
  to look at each other

Wortschatz – Textverständnis

Get connected Seite 179

E-Mails, discussion Seite 188

Unit 5 – Camden Town 3

Grammatik

- **Indirekte Fragesätze** (Reported questions) Seite 115
  I asked if you could open the door.
- **Adjektive nach Verben der Sinneswahrnehmung**
  (Adjectives after verbs of perception) Seite 99
  The cake tastes delicious.

Wortschatz – Textverständnis

German exchange Seite 193

Characterising people Seite 196

Sport Seite 171

Unit 6 – Camden Town 3

Grammatik

- **R: Conditional, type 2** Seite 63
- **R: Modal verbs and substitute forms** Seite 86
- **R:** Simple past and past progressive Seite 55
- **R: Simple past and present perfect** Seite 47

Wortschatz – Textverständnis

Holidays Seite 200

Life in the city Seite 148

Outdoor activities Seite 206

Unit 1 – English G 21 A3

Grammatik

- **The present perfect and the simple past in contrast**
  Das *present perfect* und das *simple past* im Vergleich — Seite 47

  a) **REVISION The simple past**
  Die einfache Form der Vergangenheit — Seite 43

  b) **REVISION The present perfect**
  Das *present perfect* — Seite 45

  c) **Present perfect or simple past**
  Present perfect oder *simple past* — Seite 47

- **The present perfect with *since* and *for***
  Das *present perfect* mit *since* und *for* — Seite 49
  He has been here since 4 o'clock. /
  He has been here for two hours.

- **The present perfect progressive**
  Die Verlaufsform des *present perfect* — Seite 50
  They have been waiting for a long time now.

  a) **Use** — Gebrauch

  b) **Form** — Form

Wortschatz – Textverständnis

London sights — Seite 152

Asking the way — Seite 155

Public transport — Seite 148

Unit 2 – English G 21 A3

Grammatik

- **Talking about the future** Über die Zukunft sprechen Seite 30
  - a) **The *going to*-future** Das Futur mit *going to* Seite 30
    You are going to miss the bus.
  - b) **The *will*-future** Das Futur mit *will* Seite 31
    Grandpa will be 80 this summer.
  - c) **The present progressive with future meaning**
    Das *present progressive* mit futurischer Bedeutung Seite 32
    On Saturday I am visiting my friend.
- **The *will*-future for spontaneous decisions**
  Das Futur mit *will* für spontane Entschlüsse Seite 35
  I promise I will do that.
- **Conditional sentences (type 2)** Bedingungssätze (Typ 2) Seite 63
  - a) **REVISION Conditional sentences (type 1)**
    Bedingungssätze (Typ 1) Seite 61
  - b) **Conditional sentences (type 2)**
    Bedingungssätze (Typ 2) Seite 63
    If he didn't eat the soup, his mother would be angry.

Wortschatz – Textverständnis

Town and country Seite 148

Electronic media Seite 179

Unit 3 – English G 21 A3

Grammatik

- **Relative clauses** Relativsätze Seite 124
  - a) **REVISION Relative pronouns** Relativpronomen Seite 124
    who, which, that
  - b) **Contact clauses** Relativsätze ohne Relativpronomen Seite 128
    Football is a sport I love.

• **The passive**	Das Passiv	Seite 135
The house was built by a famous architect.		
a) **Active and passive**	Aktiv und Passiv	Seite 135
b) **Form**	Form	
c) **Use**	Gebrauch	
d) **Passive sentences with *by* ...**	Passivsätze mit *by* ...	Seite 140

Wortschatz – Textverständnis

Sports and hobbies	Seite 171
Exchange student	Seite 193
Public transport	Seite 148

Unit 4 – English G 21 A3

Grammatik

• **The past perfect**	Das *past perfect*	Seite 52
When I arrived home my mother had cooked a meal.		
a) **Use**	Gebrauch	
b) **Form**	Form	
• **Talking about the past**	Über die Vergangenheit sprechen	Seite 43
a) **Simple past, past perfect, past progressive** *Simple past, past perfect, past progressive*		Seite 55
b) **Present perfect (progressive)** *Present perfect (progressive)*		Seite 50
• **Indirect speech**	Die indirekte Rede	Seite 109
a) **Direct and indirect speech** Direkte und indirekte Rede My brother says he is the best football player in town.		Seite 109
b) **Indirect speech: tense changes** Indirekte Rede: Veränderungen der Zeitform My brother said he was the best football player in town.		Seite 111

c) **Indirect speech: changes of pronouns**
Indirekte Rede: Veränderungen der Pronomen — Seite 117
He said he would call me as soon as he was at home.

Wortschatz – Textverständnis

Wildlife and nature — Seite 206

Adults and kids — Seite 217

Unit 5 – English G 21 A3

Grammatik

- **Modals and their substitutes**
  Modale Hilfsverben und ihre Ersatzverben — Seite 86

  a) **REVISION *can – may – must*** — *can – may – must* — Seite 86

  b) ***(to) be able to – (to) be allowed to – (to) have to***
  (to) be able to – (to) be allowed to – (to) have to — Seite 88
  He wasn't able to swim last year.

- **Reflexive pronouns** — Reflexivpronomen — Seite 75
  myself, yourself, …

- **Reflexive pronouns or *each other*** — Reflexivpronomen oder *each other* — Seite 79
  They are laughing at *each other*.

- **Conditional sentences (type 3)**
  Bedingungssätze (Typ 3) — Seite 66

  a) **REVISION Conditional sentences (type 1)**
  Bedingungssätze (Typ 1) — Seite 61

  b) **REVISION Conditional sentences (type 2)**
  Bedingungssätze (Typ 2) — Seite 63

  c) **Conditional sentences (type 3)**
  Bedingungssätze (Typ 3) — Seite 66
  If you had made the soup, I would have eaten it.

Wortschatz – Textverständnis

Teen magazine — Seite 184

Music — Seite 215

Unit 1 – English G access 3

Grammatik

- **The past** Die Vergangenheit Seite 43

  REVISION The simple past
  Die einfache Form der Vergangenheit Seite 43

  REVISION The present perfect
  Das *present perfect* Seite 45

  REVISION Present perfect or simple past
  Present perfect oder *simple past* Seite 47

  The present perfect progressive
  Die Verlaufsform des *present perfect* Seite 50
  He has been waiting for a long time now.

  The past perfect
  Das *past perfect* Seite 52
  She had already gone home when I arrived.

Wortschatz – Textverständnis

London attractions Seite 152

Public transport Seite 148

Unit 2 – English G access 3

Grammatik

- **The future** Das Futur Seite 30

  REVISION The *will-future*
  Das Futur mit *will* Seite 31

  REVISION The *going to-future*
  Das Futur mit *going to* Seite 30

  REVISION The present progressive: future meaning
  Das *present progressive*: futurische Bedeutung Seite 32

  The simple present: future meaning
  Das *simple present*: futurische Bedeutung Seite 34
  The train leaves at 8 o'clock.

- **Conditional sentences** Bedingungssätze Seite 61

  REVISION Conditional sentences, type 1
  Bedingungssätze, Typ 1 Seite 61

  Conditional sentences, type 2
  Bedingungssätze, Typ 2 Seite 63
  If he didn't eat the soup, his mother would be angry.

Wortschatz – Textverständnis

Town and country Seite 148

Sport Seite 171

Unit 3 – English G access 3

Grammatik

- **Relative clauses** Relativsätze Seite 124

  REVISION Relative pronouns
  Relativpronomen Seite 124
  who, which, that

  Contact clauses
  Relativsätze ohne Relativpronomen Seite 128
  Football is a sport I love.

- **The passive** Das Passiv Seite 135

  Active and passive Aktiv und Passiv Seite 135

  The passive: form Das Passiv: Form Seite 137

  Passive sentences with *by* Passivsätze mit *by* Seite 140
  The book was written by a famous author.

Wortschatz – Textverständnis

Weekend activities Seite 179

Historic sights Seite 165

Unit 4 – English G access 3

Grammatik

- **Modals and their substitutes**
  Modale Hilfsverben und ihre Ersatzverben — Seite 86

  REVISION Modal auxiliaries — Modale Hilfsverben — Seite 86

  (to) be able to* – *(to) be allowed to* – *(to) have to
  (to) be able to – *(to) be allowed to* – *(to) have to* — Seite 88
  She was able to swim when she was four.

Wortschatz – Textverständnis

Natural wonders — Seite 206

Crossing borders – Accents — Seite 196

Unit 5 – English G access 3

Grammatik

- **Reflexive pronouns** — Reflexivpronomen — Seite 75

  myself, yourself, himself, herself, itself, ourselves, yourselves, themselves
  myself, yourself, himself, herself, itself, ourselves, yourselves, themselves — Seite 75

  ***themselves* oder *each other*?**
  themselves or *each other*? — Seite 79

- **Indirect speech** — Die indirekte Rede — Seite 109

  Direct and indirect speech — Direkte und indirekte Rede — Seite 109
  He says he is in a hurry.

  Indirekte speech: tense changes
  Indirekte Rede: Veränderungen der Zeitform — Seite 111
  He said he was in a hurry.

Wortschatz – Textverständnis

Scottish traditions — Seite 161

Unusual hobby, music, entertainment — Seite 219

Unit 1 – Green Line 3 (Ausgabe 2007)

Grammatik

- **Wiederholung: Die Wiedergabe der Zukunft**
  Revision: How to express the future — Seite 30

  going to future — Seite 30

  will future — Seite 31

- **Das simple present zur Wiedergabe der Zukunft**
  The simple present to express the future — Seite 34
  The train leaves at one o'clock.

- **Das present progressive zur Wiedergabe der Zukunft**
  The present progressive to express the future — Seite 32
  I'm going on holiday next week.

- **Das *will future* zum Ausdruck von spontanen Entscheidungen**
  The will future to express spontaneous decisions — Seite 35
  I'll help you with your homework.

- **Notwendige Relativsätze**
  Defining relative clauses — Seite 125

  a) Die Relativpronomen *who, which* und *that* als Subjekt des Relativsatzes — Seite 124
  The girl who was here yesterday is my sister.

  b) Die Relativpronomen *who, which* und *that* als Objekt des Relativsatzes – *Contact clauses* — Seite 128
  The girl you met yesterday is my sister.

- **Relativsätze mit *whose***
  Relative clauses with *whose* — Seite 124

- **Präpositionen im notwendigen Relativsätze**
  Prepositions in defining relative clauses — Seite 127

Wortschatz – Textverständnis

Sport around the world — Seite 171

Sporting events — Seite 173

Agreeing and disagreeing — Seite 226

Unit 2 – Green Line 3 (Ausgabe 2007)

Grammatik

- **Wiederholung: Die modalen Hilfsverben**
  Revision: Modal auxiliaries — Seite 86

- **Die modalen Hilfsverben und ihre Ersatzverben**
  Modal auxiliaries and their substitutes — Seite 86

  a) ***can*** **und** ***be able to*** **(können)** — Seite 86
  He can swim.

  b) ***can / may, mustn't*** **und** ***be allowed*** **(dürfen)** — Seite 88
  He is allowed to swim in the lake.

  c) ***must, needn't*** **und** ***have to*** **(müssen, nicht brauchen)** — Seite 91
  He has to swim faster.

- **Das Plusquamperfekt**
  The simple past perfect — Seite 52
  When Jim came in, they had already finished the game.

Wortschatz – Textverständnis

British history — Seite 165

Writing texts using different times — Seite 167

Unit 3 – Green Line 3 (Ausgabe 2007)

Grammatik

- **Die Pronomen auf *-self / -selves*** (Reflexivpronomen)
  Self-pronouns (Reflexive pronouns) — Seite 75

  a) **Reflexiver Gebrauch** — Seite 75
  I taught myself Spanish.

  b) **Deutsch: reflexiv – englisch: nicht reflexiv** — Seite 81
  sich erinnern – to remember

  c) **Verstärkender Gebrauch** — Seite 77
  I can do it myself.

- ***Each other*** — Seite 79
  They laughed at each other.

• **Bedingungssätze**
Conditional sentences — Seite 61

a) **Typ 1 (Revision)** — Seite 61
We will go home if it rains.

b) **Typ 2** — Seite 63
If I had a lot of money, I would travel around the world.

c) **Typ 3** — Seite 66
If they had asked the teacher, they would have understood the exercise.

Wortschatz – Textverständnis

Family life and problems — Seite 217

Chatroom messages — Seite 219

Telephone messages — Seite 151

Unit 4 – Green Line 3 (Ausgabe 2007)

Grammatik

• **Der bestimmte und der unbestimmte Artikel**
The definite and the indefinite article — Seite 104

a) **Der bestimmte Artikel** — Seite 104
The music is quite loud. / I like music.

b) **Der unbestimmte Artikel** — Seite 105
He works as a dentist.

• **Das Adjektiv als Nomen**
Adjectives used as nouns — Seite 97
The rich usually live in nice houses.

• **Adjektive nach bestimmten Verben**
Adjectives after certain verbs — Seite 99
The cake tastes delicious.

• **Das Futur II**
The future perfect — Seite 36
By September they will have finished the project.

- **Paarwörter**
  Pair words — Seite 107
  glasses – pair of glasses

Wortschatz – Textverständnis

British regions — Seite 161

Help and excuses — Seite 226

Information — Seite 200

Unit 5 – Green Line 3 (Ausgabe 2007)

Grammatik

- **Das Passiv**
  The passive — Seite 135
  The classroom is cleaned every evening.
- **Vom Aktiv ins Passiv**
  From active to passive — Seite 135
- **Weitere Zeitformen des Passivs**
  Other tenses of the passive — Seite 137
- **Das Passiv bei Verben mit zwei Objekten**
  Verbs with two objects in passive sentences — Seite 139
  Pens were given to the children. /
  The children were given pens.

Wortschatz – Textverständnis

Media in your life — Seite 184

Writing a newspaper report — Seite 188

Advertising — Seite 189

Unit 6 – Green Line 3 (Ausgabe 2007)

Grammatik

- **Direkte und indirekte Rede**
  Direct and indirect speech — Seite 109
  The man says he has to go home.
- **Indirekte Rede mit Zeitverschiebung**
  Indirect speech with tense shift — Seite 111
  The man said he had to go home.
- **Zeitangaben in der indirekten Rede**
  Expressions of time in indirect speech — Seite 118
  today – that day, last year – the year before
- **Die indirekte Rede mit Einführungssatz im Präsens**
  Indirect speech with reporting verb in the present — Seite 114
- **Fragen in der indirekten Rede**
  Indirect questions — Seite 115
  She asked him when he had come home.
- **Indirekte Aufforderungssätze**
  Indirect commands — Seite 120
  She asked him to come home.

Wortschatz – Textverständnis

Travelling the world — Seite 200

Emergency report — Seite 175

Small talk — Seite 193

Unit 1 – Green Line 3 (Ausgabe 2016)

Grammatik

- **Wiederholung: Bedingungssätze Typ 1**
  Revision: Conditional sentences type 1 — Seite 61

- **Bedingungssätze Typ 2**
  Conditional sentences type 2 — Seite 63
  If I had enough money, I would travel to Australia.

- **Reflexivpronomen**
  Reflexive pronouns and *each other* — Seite 75

  a) **Reflexiver Gebrauch** — Seite 75
  I taught myself Spanish.

  b) ***Verstärkender Gebrauch*** — Seite 77
  I can do it myself.

  c) **Themselves *oder* each other** — Seite 79
  They looked at themselves in the mirror. /
  They looked at each other.

Wortschatz – Textverständnis

Different personalities — Seite 219

Themes in a story — Seite 215

Unit 2 – Green Line 3 (Ausgabe 2016)

Grammatik

- **Die Verlaufsform des Perfekts**
  The present perfect progressive — Seite 50
  I have been doing my homework for hours.

- **Das Passiv**
  The passive — Seite 135
  The classroom is cleaned every evening.

Wortschatz - Textverständnis

Scotland and its legends Seite 161

Sightsseeing Seite 152

An interview Seite 219

Unit 3 - Green Line 3 (Ausgabe 2016)

Grammatik

- **Das Plusquamperfekt**
  The past perfect simple Seite 52
  When Jim came in, they had already finished the game.

- **Bedingungssätze Typ 3**
  Conditional sentences type 3 Seite 66
  If they had asked the teacher, they would have understood the exercise.

Wortschatz - Textverständnis *In the city*
Seite 152

Historic characters and places Seite 161

Talking about history Seite 167

Intercultural meetings Seite 200

Unit 4 – Green Line 3 (Ausgabe 2016)

Grammatik

- **Aussagen in der indirekten Rede**
  Statements in indirect speech — Seite 109
  The man says he has to go home.
- **Zeit- und Ortsangaben in der indirekten Rede**
  Expressions of time and place in indirect speech — Seite 111
  today – that day, last year – the year before
- **Fragen in der indirekten Rede**
  Questions in indirect speech — Seite 115
  She asked him when he had come home.
- **Befehle, Aufforderungen und Bitten in der indirekten Rede**
  Commands and requests in indirect speech — Seite 120
  She asked him to come home.

Wortschatz – Textverständnis

Travelling and plans — Seite 196

Talking about holidays — Seite 202

GRAMMATIK

Zeitformen der Zukunft (*The future tenses*)

1 Das Futur mit *going to* (*The going to-future*)

●○○ 1. Sieh dir die Bilder an. Was wird hier gleich passieren?
Schreibe ganze Sätze mit *going to*.

→ Lösung S. 40

a) It ______________________ (rain)   b) He ______________________ (win)

c) They ______________________ (fall)   d) She ______________________ (miss)

●○○ 2. Ergänze die Sätze mit dem *going to-future*.

→ Lösung S. 40

buy • give • go • have • post • visit

a) We ______________________ a barbecue on Saturday afternoon.

b) I ______________________ these photos online when I get home.

c) My parents ______________________ me a new bike for my birthday.

d) ________ you ______________________ Rome while you are in Italy?

e) We ______________________ swimming later.

f) I ______________________ a new app with my pocket money.

2. Das Futur mit *will* (*The will-future*)

●○○ 1. Ergänze diese Sätze mit dem *will-future* und den Angaben, die in Klammern stehen.

→ Lösung S. 40

a) How old ______________________ on his next birthday? (your brother / be)

b) Germany ______________________ against France in the next match. (play)

c) The weather report says that it ______________________ at the weekend. (snow)

d) We ______________________ for a run if it's still raining. (not / go)

e) ______________________ on the moon in the year 3000? (people / live)

f) No, I ______________________ you with your homework. (not / help)

g) Theresa ______________________ us the link later today. (send)

h) Tim ______________________ this photo. Please use a different one. (not / like)

i) ______________________ at me? (your dog / bark)

j) You ______________________ better if you drink some water. (feel)

●○○ 2. Das *will-future* kann auch eine Vermutung ausdrücken. Verbinde die passenden Satzteile.

→ Lösung S. 40

a) I promise I will clean	time for an ice-cream this afternoon.
b) They hope it won't rain	a great holiday!
c) Do you think there will be	my room later!
d) Maybe we will have	on the day of the match.
e) I'm sure John will like	me his skateboard?
f) We hope you will have	a German test tomorrow?
g) Do you think Paul will lend	his birthday present.

3 Das *present progressive* mit futurischer Bedeutung (*The present progressive with future meaning*)

●○○ 1. Hier ist Maries Kalender für die nächste Woche. Schreibe ihre Termine in ganzen Sätzen auf und verwende dabei das *present progressive*.

→ Lösung S. 40

Monday:	swimming club
Tuesday:	lunch with Paul at La Venezia
Wednesday:	basketball training
Thursday:	revise for maths test!
Friday:	watch new Star Wars film

a) *Marie is going to the swimming club on Monday.*

b) ______________________________

c) ______________________________

d) ______________________________

e) ______________________________

●○○ 2. Bilde Sätze aus den angegebenen Wörtern. Verwende dabei das *present progressive*.

→ Lösung S. 40

a) my parents / buy / new car / weekend

____

b) he / post / new video / 2 o'clock

____

c) you / come / to Jack's party?

____

d) they / not go / on holiday / this summer

____

●○○ 3. Ergänze den Dialog mit dem richtigen Verb im *present progressive*.

→ Lösung S. 40

camp • do • fly • go • have • stay

Julia: What a) are you doing ______________ in the summer holidays, Jack?

Jack: Oh, not much. I b) ______________ with my grandparents in Bath for a week. Then my parents and I c) ______________ on Dartmoor for a few days in a big tent. What about you?

Julia: Oh, we d) ______________ to Florida for two weeks! We e) ______________ to Disney World and the Kennedy Space Center while we're there. I can't wait!

Jack: Sounds great!

Julia: Yes, it will be. But before we go, I f) ______________ ______________ extra maths lessons every day for two weeks!

Jack: Oh, bad luck!

4 Das *simple present* mit futurischer Bedeutung (*The simple present with future meaning*)

●○○ 1. Bilde Sätze im *simple present* wie in dem Beispiel. → Lösung S. 41

a) airport bus – leave station – 11.20

The airport bus leaves the station at 11.20.

b) film – start – 7 p.m.

____

c) English lesson – finish – quarter past 10

____

d) match – begin – half past 3

____

e) train – arrive – 2.55

____

●○○ 2. Welche Fragen passen zu den gegebenen Antworten? → Lösung S. 41

a) ____?

The swimming lesson ends at quarter to 5.

b) ____?

Angela's plane arrives at 3.15 tomorrow afternoon.

c) ____?

School starts at 8.15 next Monday.

d) ____?

The concert begins at 7 o'clock.

e) ____?

The supermarket opens at half past 7.

5 Das Futur mit *will* für spontane Entschlüsse (*The will-future for spontaneous decisions*)

●○○ 1. Welche beiden Sätze passen zusammen? Verbinde. → Lösung S. 41

a) There's no milk.
d) Oh no! I've broken Mia's phone!
c) Tim is thirsty.
f) These boxes are very heavy.
b) I don't understand this exercise.
e) It's very hot in this room.
h) That TV show is boring.
g) I need to speak to Judy.

I'll open the window.
Don't worry. I won't tell her.
I'll buy some at the supermarket.
I'll phone her later.
I'll explain it to you.
Really? I won't watch it, then.
I'll help you carry them.
I'll give him a glass of water.

●○○ 2. Diese Sätze mit spontanen Entschlüssen müssen mit dem *will-future* ergänzt werden. → Lösung S. 41

ask • correct • do • eat • feed • give • go • post

a) These are great photos! I ________________ them online this evening.

b) I ________________ you my e-mail address, then you can contact me.

c) I'm tired. I think I ________________ to bed early tonight.

d) Oh! This answer is wrong. I ________________ it.

e) The dog is hungry. I ________________ it now.

f) I want to watch TV now, so I ________________ my homework later.

g) "Who wants the last cookie?" "I ________________ it!"

h) Sorry, I don't know the answer. I ________________ Mark.

6 Das Futur II (*The future perfect*)

●○○ 1. Sylvie hat große Pläne für nächstes Jahr. Schreibe auf, was sie gemacht haben wird, wenn alles nach ihrem Plan verläuft. Schreibe im *future perfect*.

→ Lösung S. 41

My 6-month plan for becoming a star:

January: write a hit song

February: upload the song

March: get a million fans

April: make a CD

May: win a big music prize

June: become very rich

a) By the end of January, she'll have written a hit song.

b) ______

c) ______

d) ______

e) ______

f) ______

●○○ 2. Schreibe Sätze im *future perfect*. Verwende das Verb in Klammern.

→ Lösung S. 41

a) By the end of this year, we ______ (learn) lots of new English words.

b) Kate ______ (not / finish) her homework by this evening.

c) They ______ (drink) all the cola by the end of the party.

d) I won't be here at 6 p.m. I ______ (leave) by then.

e) ______ you ______ (watch) my new video by tomorrow morning?

7 Gemischte Aufgaben (*Mixed forms*)

●○○ 1. Plan oder spontane Entscheidung?
Ergänze die Sätze mit der richtigen Verbform. → Lösung S. 42

a) It's going to rain later. ______ my umbrella with me.

☐ I'm taking ☐ I'll take

b) ______ to the cinema on Saturday evening.

☐ We're going ☐ We'll go

c) I want to watch this video now. ______ my room later.

☐ I'm cleaning ☐ I'll clean

d) "I don't know where the cafeteria is." "Come with me. ______ you."

☐ I'm showing ☐ I'll show

e) Jonas ______ us at the station at half past seven.

☐ is meeting ☐ will meet

f) Sorry, I can't come with you tomorrow. I ______ basketball at that time.

☐ am playing ☐ will play

●●○ 2. *Present simple* oder *present progressive*? → Lösung S. 42

a) The film ______________ (begin) at 7 o'clock – we mustn't be late!

b) We ______________ (not / have) a maths test tomorrow. It's on Friday.

c) ______________ you ______________ (go) to the concert this weekend?

d) When ______________ the train ______________ (arrive) in Munich?

e) This German lesson is so long! It ______________ (not / finish) until 2.30!

f) We ______________ (move) house next week. It's very exciting!

●○○ 3. Was passt besser in die Lücke – die Form von *will* oder die Form von *going to*? → Lösung S. 42

a) Anna is putting her tennis racket in her bag. She ______________ play tennis this afternoon.

b) Who do you think ______________ be the next President?

c) We hope we ______________ see you at the meeting this afternoon.

d) When I get home, I ______________ have a bath and go to bed early.

e) It's Charlie's birthday tomorrow, so I ______________ buy him a present.

f) We're very excited because we ______________ get a dog!

g) I promise I ______________ phone you as soon as I get home.

h) Oh no! I forgot to send Ben the e-mail. I ______________ do it now.

i) Jamie's sister ______________ have a baby in November.

j) "I don't know how to upload photos on this phone."
"I ______________ show you."

●●○ 4. Verwende das *going to-future* oder das *will-future* und ergänze das richtige Verb. → Lösung S. 42

buy • not / cook • invite • lose • take

a) My grandma is in hospital, so I ______________ her some flowers.

b) Don't lend Mick your phone! I'm sure he ______________ it.

c) I think I ______________ Emma to have coffee with me. She seems very nice!

d) Mum ______________ lunch for us on Saturday. We're going to a restaurant instead.

e) Lizzie ______________ lots of photos at the party and send us copies.

●●○ 5. Kontrolliere die Futurformen in den Sätzen.
Korrigiere die Fehler. Einer der Sätze ist ohne Fehler. → Lösung S. 42

a) What time is the next bus leaving?

____

b) Wait a minute! I'm going to open the door for you.

____

c) Tony is flying to Paris on Saturday.

____

d) We'll go to the lake this afternoon. Do you want to come?

____

e) Luke has got sugar, flour, butter and eggs. He'll make a cake.

____

f) I think people are flying to Mars in about 50 years from now.

____

●●○ 6. Ergänze die Sätze mit dem angegebenen Verb.
Verwende die Form des Futurs, die am besten passt. → Lösung S. 42

a) I __________________ (empty) the dishwasher for you, Mum!

b) We need to learn these words – we __________________ (have) a test next week.

c) Be careful! You __________________ (fall)!

d) School __________________ (start) at 8 a.m. Why are you always late?

e) There __________________ (be) a lot of rain this morning, then some sun in the afternoon.

f) We __________________ (watch) the film at Jack's house this evening.

1 Das Futur mit *going to* (*The going to-future*)

Übungen ab S. 30

1. a) It's going to rain. b) He's going to win. c) They're going to fall. d) She's going to miss the train.

2. a) We **are going to have** a barbecue on Saturday afternoon. b) I**'m going to post** these photos online when I get home. c) My parents **are going to give** me a new bike for my birthday. d) **Are** you **going to visit** Rome while you are in Italy? e) We **are going to go** swimming later. f) I **am going to buy** a new app with my pocket money.

2 Das Futur mit *will* (*The will-future*)

Übungen ab S. 31

1. a) How old **will your brother be** on his next birthday? b) Germany **will play** against France in the next match. c) The weather report says that it **will snow** at the weekend. d) We **won't go** for a run if it's still raining. e) **Will people live** on the moon in the year 3000? f) No, I **won't help** you with your homework. g) Theresa **will send** us the link later today. h) Tim **won't like** this photo. Please use a different one. i) **Will your dog bark** at me? j) You **will feel** better if you drink some water.

2. a) I promise I will clean **my room later**! b) They hope it won't rain **on the day of the match**. c) Do you think there will be **a German test tomorrow**? d) Maybe we will have **time for an ice-cream this afternoon**. e) I'm sure John will like **his birthday presen**t. f) We hope you will have **a great holiday**! g) Do you think Paul will lend **me his skateboard**?

3 Das *present progressive* mit futurischer Bedeutung (*The present progressive with future meaning*)

Übungen ab S. 32

1. b) Marie is having lunch with Paul at La Venezia on Tuesday. c) Marie is going to basketball training on Wednesday. d) Marie is revising for a maths test on Thursday. e) Marie is watching the new Star Wars film on Friday.

2. a) My parents are buying a new car at the weekend. b) He is posting a new video at 2 o'clock. c) Are you coming to Jack's party? d) They aren't going on holiday this summer.

3. *Julia:* What a) **are you doing** in the summer holidays, Jack?
   Jack: Oh, not much. I b) **am staying** with my grandparents in Bath for a week. Then my parents and I c) **are camping** on Dartmoor for a few days in a big tent. What about you?
   Julia: Oh, we d) **are flying** to Florida for two weeks! We e) **are going** to Disney World and the Kennedy Space Center while we're there. I can't wait!
   Jack: Sounds great!
   Julia: Yes, it will be. But before we go, I f) **am having** extra maths lessons every day for 2 weeks!
   Jack: Oh, bad luck!

4 Das *simple present* mit futurischer Bedeutung (*The simple present with future meaning*)

Übungen ab S. 34

1. b) The film starts at 7 p.m. c) The English lesson finishes at quarter past 10. d) The match begins at half past 3. e) The train arrives at 2.55.

2. a) What time / When does the swimming lesson end? b) What time / When does Angela's plane arrive? c) What time / When does school start next Monday? d) What time / When does the concert begin? e) What time / When does the supermarket open?

5 Das Futur mit *will* für spontane Entschlüsse (*The will-future for spontaneous decisions*)

Übungen ab S. 35

1. a) There's no milk. I'll buy some at the supermarket. b) I don't understand this exercise. I'll explain it to you. c) Tim is thirsty. I'll give him a glass of water. d) Oh no! I've broken Mia's phone! Don't worry. I won't tell her. e) It's very hot in this room. I'll open the window. f) These boxes are very heavy. I'll help you carry them. g) I need to speak to Judy. I'll phone her later. h) That TV show is boring. Really? I won't watch it, then.

2. a) These are great photos! **I'll post** them online this evening. b) **I'll give** you my e-mail address, then you can contact me. c) I'm tired. I think **I'll go** to bed early tonight. d) Oh! This answer is wrong. **I'll correct** it. e) The dog is hungry. **I'll feed** it now. f) I want to watch TV now, so **I'll do** my homework later. g) "Who wants the last cookie?" "**I'll eat** it!" h) Sorry, I don't know the answer. **I'll ask** Mark.

6 Das Futur II (*The future perfect*)

Übungen ab S. 36

1. b) By the end of February, she'll have uploaded the song. c) By the end of March, she'll have got a million fans. d) By the end of April, she'll have made a CD. e) By the end of May, she'll have won a big music prize. f) By the end of June, she'll have become very rich.

2. a) By the end of this year, **we'll have learned** lots of new English words. b) Kate **won't have finished** her homework by this evening. c) They **will have drunk** all the cola by the end of the party. d) I won't be here at 6 p.m. **I'll have left** by then. e) **Will you have watched** my new video by tomorrow morning?

7 Gemischte Aufgaben (*Mixed forms*)

Übungen ab S. 37

1. a) It's going to rain later. **I'll take** my umbrella with me. b) **We're going** to the cinema on Saturday evening. c) I want to watch this video now. **I'll clean** my room later. d) "I don't know where the cafeteria is." "Come with me. **I'll show** you." e) Jonas **is meeting** us at the station at half past seven. f) Sorry, I can't come with you tomorrow. **I'm playing** basketball at that time.

2. a) The film **begins** at 7 o'clock – we mustn't be late! b) We **aren't having** a maths test tomorrow. It's on Friday. c) **Are** you **going** to the concert this weekend? d) When **does** the train **arrive** in Munich? e) This German lesson is so long! It **doesn't finish** until 2.30! f) We **are moving** house next week. It's very exciting!

3. a) Anna is putting her tennis racket in her bag. She **is going to** play tennis this afternoon. b) Who do you think **will** be the next President? c) We hope we **will** see you at the meeting this afternoon. d) When I get home, I **am going** to have a bath and go to bed early. e) It's Charlie's birthday tomorrow, so I **am going to** buy him a present. f) We're very excited because we **are going to** get a dog! g) I promise I **will** phone you as soon as I get home. h) Oh no! I forgot to send Ben the e-mail. I **will** do it now. i) Jamie's sister **is going to** have a baby in November. j) "I don't know how to upload photos on this phone." "I **will** show you."

4. a) My grandma is in hospital, so I **am going to buy** her some flowers. b) Don't lend Mick your phone! I'm sure he **will lose** it. c) I think I **will invite** Emma to have coffee with me. She seems very! d) Mum **isn't going to cook** lunch for us on Saturday. We're going to a restaurant instead. e) Lizzie **is going to take** lots of photos at the party and send us copies.

5. a) What time **does** the next bus **leave**? b) Wait a minute! **I'll open** the door for you. c) ☑ d) **We're going** to the lake this afternoon. Do you want to come? e) Luke has got sugar, flour, butter and eggs. **He's going to make** a cake. f) I think people **will fly** to Mars in about 50 years from now.

6. a) I **will empty** the dishwasher for you, Mum! b) We need to learn these words – we **are having** a test next week. c) Be careful! You **are going to fall**! d) School **starts** at 8 a.m. Why are you always late? e) There **will be** a lot of rain this morning, then some sun in the afternoon. f) We **are watching** the film at Jack's house this evening.

Zeitformen der Vergangenheit (*The past tenses*)

1 Die einfache Vergangenheit (*The simple past*)

●○○ 1. Welches Verb passt in die Lücken?
Verwende das *simple past*. → Lösung S. 57

cost • drive • fly • give • go • have • sell • win

a) I flew to Rome with my family last summer.

b) Tom and Simon went swimming in the sea.

c) The concert tickets cost a lot of money.

d) We gave our aunt some beautiful flowers.

e) He drove to the hotel in his new red car.

f) I can't believe it! Our team won the match!

g) They sold their house in London and moved to the countryside.

h) We had a really nice holiday!

●○○ 2. Schreibe Sätze im *simple past*. Verwende in einem Satz immer dasselbe Verb – einmal bejaht und einmal verneint. → Lösung S. 57

a) They *ate* all the ice-cream but they *didn't eat* the salad. (eat)

b) I saw you yesterday but you didn't see me. (see)

c) The thieves took my bike but they didn't take my skateboard. (take)

d) Jim bought new shoes but he didn't buy a jacket. (buy)

e) Clare told Jenny about the party but she didn't tell Anna. (tell)

f) I forgot my keys but I didn't forget my phone. (forget)

3. Hier haben sich Fehler eingeschlichen.
Finde und verbessere sie.

Lösung S. 57

a) They didn't understood the question.

They didn't understand the question

b) Thomas gone out 10 minutes ago.

c) What did you yesterday in the geography lesson?

d) She is a very slow runner. She did lose the race.

e) Mrs Dillon teached us some new grammar.

f) These shoes costed a lot of money.

4. Übersetze diese Sätze ins Englische.
Verwende das *simple past*.

Lösung S. 57

a) Ich habe Maria gestern in der Stadt getroffen.

b) Wo hast du vor fünf Jahren gewohnt?

c) Sie hat mir ihre Telefonnummer gegeben.

d) Jake hat uns nicht gesehen.

2. Das *present perfect* (*The present perfect*)

●○○ 1. Vervollständige diese Sätze mit den in Klammern angegebenen Verben im *present perfect*.

→ Lösung S. 57

a) I hope you have had a nice day. (have)

b) Has the film begun yet? (begin)

c) Helen has hurt her leg. She can't walk at the moment. (hurt)

d) No, I haven't ridden a horse before! (not / ride)

e) Harry has worn that T-shirt every day this week! He stinks! (wear)

f) Have you ever written a letter with a pen and paper? (write)

g) Oh dear. Carla hasn't found her keys yet. (not / find)

●○○ 2. Bilde ganze Sätze im *present perfect*.

→ Lösung S. 57

a) Paul / never be / Scotland

Paul has never been to Scotland.

b) they / not / take / a lot of photos / today

They haven't taken...

c) you / read / all of / "Harry Potter" / books?

Have you read ...

d) Linda / jog / 8 kilometres / this week

Linda has

e) anybody / see / my phone?

Have anybody seen my phone?

f) they / not / finish / all the exercises / yet

They havent finished ...

●○○ 3. Das *present perfect* wird oft zusammen mit Adverbien der unbestimmten Zeit verwendet. Welches Adverb passt in welchen Satz?

→ Lösung S. 57

already • always • before • ever • just • never • often • yet

a) Have you ever swum in the Atlantic Ocean?

b) No, I haven't been to Hamburg before. It's my first visit.

c) We're not hungry. We've ~~already~~ just had lunch.

d) I've ~~often~~ already seen this film. Let's watch a different one.

e) Cathy has always dreamed of being a pop star.

f) Have you learnt all the new English words yet ?

g) Our grandfather has ~~just~~ often told us stories about his life.

h) No, I've never eaten Japanese food. Does it taste good?

●●○ 4. Jeder Satz erzählt eine Situation. Verwende die Wörter, die in der Klammer stehen, um zu erklären, was vorher passiert ist.

→ Lösung S. 57

a) There is no more cake. (children / eat)

The children have eaten all the cake.

b) Nicola doesn't have any more pocket money. (spend)

____

c) Lily isn't here now. (go / home)

____

d) Christopher doesn't have any more homework today. (finish)

____

e) I don't need to read this book. (already / read)

____

3 Das *simple past* und das *present perfect* im Vergleich (*The simple past and present perfect in contrast*)

●○○ 1. Füge die richtige Verbform ein. Überlege dabei, ob das Geschehen abgeschlossen ist (*simple past*) oder ob es noch andauert (*present perfect*).

→ Lösung S. 58

a) We went to Scotland on holiday last summer. (go)

b) Have you seen Caroline today? Is she here? (see)

c) They have just started a new unit in their English book. (start)

d) I first met Lisa three years ago. (meet)

e) "What's that noise?" "It's my phone. Someone has sent me a new message." (send)

f) Matthew got up at 1 p.m. last Saturday! He's so lazy! (get up)

g) She didn't understand what I said, so I repeated it. (not / understand)

h) Mr Collins has come all the way from Edinburgh to speak to us today. (come)

●○○ 2. Markiere die richtige Verbform.

→ Lösung S. 58

a) Where have you been / did you go on your last holiday?

b) I've never eaten / I never ate Korean food.

c) The team has won / won all their matches so far this year.

d) Melanie has learned / learned to swim when she was 7.

e) Dad, how much coffee have you drunk / did you drink today?

f) My dad hasn't slept / didn't sleep last night because he drank too much coffee!

●○○ 3. Kreuze die Verbform an, die am besten passt. → Lösung S. 58

a) I'm a bit nervous because ______ before.

☐ I never flew ☐ I've never flown

b) ______ your room yet?

☐ Did you clean ☐ Have you cleaned

c) ______ at the weekend?

☐ What did you do ☐ What have you done

d) I can't find my phone! I think someone ______ it!

☐ stole ☐ has stolen

e) Ben ______ to school last week.

☐ didn't go ☐ hasn't gone

f) "Where's Ellie?" "I don't know. She ______ here a few minutes ago."

☐ was ☐ has been

●●○ 4. Finde die Satzteile, die zusammenpassen. → Lösung S. 58

a) No, we didn't have	She doesn't live here now.
b) No, we haven't had	couldn't get into the house.
c) Kate moved to Spain	a test last week.
d) Kate has moved to Spain.	at school yesterday?
e) I forgot my keys and	two years ago.
f) I've forgotten my keys!	today? Tim is looking for him.
g) Did you see Tony	a test this week.
h) Have you seen Tony	I can't get into the house!

4 Das *present perfect* mit *since* und *for* (*The present perfect with since and for*)

●○○ 1. Ergänze die Sätze mit *since* oder *for*. → Lösung S. 58

a) We've been at school ______________ 8 o'clock this morning.

b) She's had her new phone ______________ September.

c) I haven't spoken to Tina ______________ three days.

d) They've lived in Frankfurt ______________ 2014.

e) Harry hasn't eaten meat ______________ six months.

f) The church has stood here ______________ three hundred years.

g) I've known Clara ______________ the day we started school.

h) It's rained every day ______________ more than a week.

●○○ 2. Beantworte die Fragen mit den Angaben in der Klammer und ergänze *since* oder *for*. → Lösung S. 58

a) How long have you worked here? (last January)

____

b) How long has Charlotte been ill? (three days)

____

c) How long has your brother had a tattoo? (he was 18)

____

d) How long have you known about Dylan's party? (Thursday)

____

e) How long have you been here? (five minutes)

____

5 Die Verlaufsform des *present perfect* (*The present perfect progressive*)

●○○ 1. Schreibe Sätze zu den Bildern im *present perfect progressive*.

→ Lösung S. 59

a) They ______________ (play)

b) ______________ (eat)

c) ______________ (sleep)

d) ______________ (jogging)

●○○ 2. Ergänze das richtige Verb und setze es ins *present perfect progressive*.

→ Lösung S. 59

chat • learn • lie • play • not / wait • watch

a) I ______________ this game for hours but I can't get to the next level.

b) Chrissie ______________ to her friends since she got home.

c) How long __________ you ______________ English?

d) You ______________ TV all afternoon! Please switch it off now.

e) "Sorry I'm late." "It's OK. We ______________ for very long."

f) The cat ______________ in the sun all day.

●●○ 3. Bilde Sätze im *present perfect progressive*. → Lösung S. 59

a) the girls / walk / around city / all afternoon

____

b) it / snow / a lot / this week

____

c) how long / you / go / to this school?

____

d) you / not listen / to me

____

e) I / play / guitar / 5 years

____

●●○ 4. Verben, die Zustände beschreiben, werden generell nicht in der Verlaufsform verwendet. Markiere die richtige Verbform in diesen Sätzen. → Lösung S. 59

a) I have always loved / have always been loving Chinese food.

b) We have studied / have been studying Roman Britain for the last three weeks.

c) How long have you known / have you been knowing Patricia?

d) How long have we waited / have we been waiting for the bus?

e) I have called / have been calling Gracie all day but she hasn't answered her phone yet.

f) Have you remembered / Have you been remembering to bring the key?

g) Martin is very hot. He has run / has been running around in the sun.

6 Das Plusquamperfekt (*The past perfect*)

●○○ 1. Ergänze die Sätze mit dem richtigen Verb und verwende das *past perfect*.

→ Lösung S. 59

cut • not / eat • finish • start • stop • take

a) I didn't need to do any homework last Sunday. I ____________ already ________________ it.

b) We were late. The lesson ________________ when we arrived.

c) Lena was hungry in the evening because she ________________ all day.

d) Our neighbour, Mr Baxter, thanked me because I ________________ his grass for him.

e) Flynn posted some of the photos he ________________ on his social media page.

f) They went for a walk after it ________________ raining.

●○○ 2. *Positive* oder *negative*? Verwende die richtige Form des *past perfect*.

→ Lösung S. 59

a) Donna ________________ us before, so we took her on a tour of the city. (visit)

b) Pat ________________ his key, so he couldn't open the door. (lose)

c) Marie was in trouble yesterday because she ________________ to do her geography homework. (forget)

d) I ________________ my messages, so I didn't know what time we were meeting. (check)

e) We didn't know where Karen was. We ________________ her all day. (see)

●●○ 3. Sieh die Bilder an und entscheide, ob du das Verb im *simple past* oder *past perfect* verwenden musst. → Lösung S. 59

a) When we arrived home, Dad _____________ (*cook*) the dinner.

b) When my phone _____________ (*ring*), I answered it.

c) When Linda fell over, she _____________ (*hurt*) her knee.

d) When he got to the shop, it _____________ (*closed*).

●●○ 4. Bilde Sätze aus den Stichwörtern. Verwende das *simple past* oder das *past perfect*. → Lösung S. 59

a) after / Nick win the Oscar / everyone know / his name

After Nick had won the Oscar, everyone knew his name.

b) I / go for a run / as soon as / stop raining

____

c) Simon / be late / because / not hear / his alarm clock

____

d) I / not see / post / Justine / write

____

7 Das *past progressive* (*The past progressive*)

●○○ 1. Ergänze die Sätze mit dem richtigen Verb im *past progressive*.

→ Lösung S. 60

do • not / feel • go • lie • live • play • start • wait • not / watch

a) At 3 o'clock yesterday afternoon, Chris ______________________ his new computer game.

b) Two years ago, I ______________________ in Berlin.

c) Where ______________ you ______________________ when I saw you on Saturday morning?

d) At this time last week, we ______________________ on the beach in Spain.

e) No, I __________________ TV! I __________________ my homework!

f) They ______________________ for their teacher in Room 34, but the lesson was in Room 36.

g) One year ago, we ______________________ to learn French.

h) Gina went home because she ______________________ well.

●○○ 2. Formuliere Antworten, zu den gestellten Fragen. Verwende dabei die *schräg* gedruckten Wörter.

→ Lösung S. 60

a) What were you doing on the bus this morning? *finish / homework*

____

b) What was Helen wearing at Ben's party? *jeans and T-shirt*

____

c) Where were you going last Friday evening? *meet / friends / cinema*

____

d) What were you doing at 6 o'clock this morning? *sleep*

____

8 Das *simple past* und das *past progressive* (*The simple past and the past progressive*)

●○○ 1. Verbinde die Satzteile, die zusammenpassen. → Lösung S. 60

a) Jane fell over because	I took off my jacket.
b) Our team was losing when	when the teacher came into the room.
c) When I saw Mark,	when he fell and broke his leg.
d) I was feeling hot, so	she was looking at her phone.
e) We were waiting at the bus stop	I heard my favourite song.
f) Liam was skateboarding	while it was running through the grass.
g) While I was listening to the radio,	John scored a goal.
h) The cat caught a mouse	he was talking to Pete's girlfriend.
i) The children were shouting	when it started to rain.

●●○ 2. Füge die Verben ein. Überlege dabei, ob das Verb die Atmosphäre vorgibt (*past progressive*) oder einzelne Ereignisse beschreibt (*simple past*). → Lösung S. 60

It a) ________________ (be) a cold day in the middle of winter. An icy wind b) ________________ (blow) and snow c) ________________ (start) to fall. People d) ________________ (hurry) home to get inside, away from the cold air.

Tom e) ________________ (go) home, too. He f) ________________ (not / want) to miss his favourite TV show. Suddenly he g) ________________ (hear) someone shout: "Stop that man! He's stolen my rucksack!" Tom h) ________________ (look) around. A man i) ________________ (run) towards him. He j) ________________ (hold) a green rucksack.

●●○ 3. Wähle für jeden Satz die richtige Zeitform. → Lösung S. 60

a) I ______ my e-mails when I got a text from Claire.
☐ checked ☐ was checking

b) When I saw Mrs Miller at the train station, I ______ hello.
☐ said ☐ was saying

c) Matt burnt his mouth while he ______ very hot tea.
☐ drank ☐ was drinking

d) I found some money when I ______ my dog in the park.
☐ walked ☐ was walking

e) Zoe was surprised when Lisa ______ her a birthday card.
☐ sent ☐ was sending

f) When we got up that morning, the sun ______ .
☐ shone ☐ was shining

●●○ 4. Ergänze die Sätze mit der richtigen Vergangenheitsform. → Lösung S. 60

a) When the lesson ____________________ (end), the children ____________________ (close) their books.

b) Sean ____________________ (do) his homework when his computer ____________________ (crash).

c) The accident ____________________ (happen) because Andy ____________________ (drive) too fast.

d) When the accident ____________________ (happen), somebody ____________________ (call) the police.

e) I ____________________ (not / hear) you because ____________________ (talk) on the phone.

f) Pat ____________________ (lose) a tooth when the ball ____________________ (hit) his face.

1 Die einfache Vergangenheit (*The simple past*)

Übungen ab S. 43

1. a) I **flew** to Rome with my family last summer. b) Tom and Simon **went** swimming in the sea. c) The concert tickets **cost** a lot of money. d) We **gave** our aunt some beautiful flowers. e) He **drove** to the hotel in his new red car. f) I can't believe it! Our team **won** the match! g) They **sold** their house in London and moved to the countryside. h) We **had** a really nice holiday!

2. b) I **saw** you yesterday but you **didn't see** me. c) The thieves **took** my bike but they **didn't take** my skateboard. d) Jim **bought** new shoes but he **didn't buy** a jacket. e) Clare **told** Jenny about the party but she **didn't tell** Anna. f) I **forgot** my keys but I **didn't forget** my phone.

3. a) They didn't **understand** the question. b) Thomas **went** out 10 minutes ago. c) What did you **do** yesterday in the geography lesson? d) She is a very slow runner. She **lost** the race. e) Mrs Dillon **taught** us some new grammar. f) These shoes **cost** a lot of money.

4. a) I met Maria in the city / town yesterday. b) Where did you live five years ago? c) She gave me her phone number. d) Jake didn't see us.

2 Das *present perfect* (*The present perfect*)

Übungen ab S. 45

1. a) I hope you **have had** a nice day. b) **Has** the film **begun** yet? c) Helen **has hurt** her leg. She can't walk at the moment. d) No, I **haven't ridden** a horse before! e) Harry **has worn** that T-shirt every day this week! He stinks! f) **Have** you ever **written** a letter with a pen and paper? g) Oh dear. Carla **hasn't found** her keys yet.

2. a) Paul has never been to Scotland. b) They haven't taken a lot of photos today. c) Have you read all of the "Harry Potter" books? d) Linda has jogged 8 kilometres this week. e) Has anybody seen my phone? f) They haven't finished all the exercises yet.

3. a) Have you **ever** swum in the Atlantic Ocean? b) No, I haven't been to Hamburg **before**. It's my first visit. c) We're not hungry. We've **just** had lunch. d) I've **already** seen this film. Let's watch a different one. e) Cathy has **always** dreamed of being a pop star. f) Have you learnt all the new English words **yet**? g) Our grandfather has **often** told us stories about his life. h) No, I've **never** eaten Japanese food. Does it taste good?

4. b) Nicola has spent her pocket money. c) Lily has gone home. d) Christopher has finished his homework. e) I've already read it.

3 Das *simple past* und das *present perfect* im Vergleich (*The simple past and present perfect in contrast*)

Übungen ab S. 47

1. a) We **went** to Scotland on holiday last summer. b) **Have** you **seen** Caroline today? Is she here? c) They **have** just **started** a new unit in their English book. d) I first **met** Lisa three years ago. e) "What's that noise?" "It's my phone. Someone **has sent** me a new message." f) Matthew **got up** at 1 p.m. last Saturday! He's so lazy! g) She **didn't understand** what I said, so I repeated it. h) Mr Collins **has come** all the way from Edinburgh to speak to us today.

2. a) **Where did you go** on your last holiday? b) **I've never eaten** Korean food. c) The team **has won** all their matches so far this year. d) Melanie **learned** to swim when she was 7. e) Dad, how much coffee **have you drunk** today? f) My dad **didn't sleep** last night because he drank too much coffee!

3. a) I'm a bit nervous because **I've never flown** before. b) **Have you cleaned** your room yet? c) **What did you do** at the weekend? d) I can't find my phone! I think someone **has stolen** it! e) Ben **didn't go** to school last week. f) "Where's Ellie?" "I don't know. She **was** here a few minutes ago."

4. a) No we didn't have a test last week. b) No, we haven't had a test this week. c) Kate moved to Spain two years ago. d) Kate has moved to Spain. She doesn't live here now. e) I forgot my keys and couldn't get into the house. f) I've forgotten my keys! I can't get into the house! g) Did you see Tony at school yesterday? h) Have you seen Tony today? Tim is looking for him.

4 Das *present perfect* mit *since* oder *for* (*The present perfect with since or for*)

Übungen ab S. 49

1. a) We've been at school **since** 8 o'clock this morning. b) She's had her new phone **since** September. c) I haven't spoken to Tina **for** three days. d) They've lived in Frankfurt **since** 2014. e) Harry hasn't eaten meat **for** six months. f) The church has stood here **for** three hundred years. g) I've known Clara **since** the day we started school. h) It's rained every day **for** more than a week.

2. a) I've worked here **since** last January. b) Charlotte has been ill **for** three days. c) He's had a tattoo **since** he was 18. d) I've known about Dylan's party **since** Thursday. e) I've been here **for** five minutes.

5 Die Verlaufsform des present perfect (*The present perfect progressive*)

→ Übungen ab S. 50

1. a) They've been playing football. b) He has been eating chocolate. c) The cat has been sleeping. f) She's been jogging.

2. a) I **have been playing** this game for hours but I can't get to the next level. b) Chrissie **has been chatting** to her friends since she got home. c) How long **have** you **been learning** English? d) You **have been watching** TV all afternoon! Please switch it off now. e) "Sorry I'm late." "It's OK. We **haven't been waiting** for very long." f) The cat **has been lying** in the sun all day.

3. a) The girls have been walking around the city all afternoon. b) It has been snowing a lot this week. c) How long have you been going to this school? d) You haven't been listening to me. e) I've been playing the guitar for 5 years.

4. a) I **have always loved** Chinese food. b) We **have been studying** Roman Britain for the last three weeks. c) How long **have you known** Patricia? d) How long **have we been waiting** for the bus? e) I **have been calling** Gracie all day but she hasn't answered her phone yet. f) **Have you remembered** to bring the key? g) Martin is very hot. He **has been running** around in the sun.

6 Das Plusquamperfekt (*The past perfect*)

→ Übungen ab S. 52

1. a) I didn't need to do any homework last Sunday. I **had** already **finished** it. b) We were late. The lesson **had started** when we arrived. c) Lena was hungry in the evening because she **hadn't eaten** all day. d) Our neighbour, Mr Baxter, thanked me because I **had cut** his grass for him. e) Flynn posted some of the photos he **had taken** on his social media page. f) They went for a walk after it **had stopped** raining.

2. a) Donna **hadn't visited** us before, so we took her on a tour of the city. b) Pat **had lost** his key, so he couldn't open the door. c) Marie was in trouble yesterday because she **had forgotten** to do her geography homework. d) I **hadn't checked** my messages, so I didn't know what time we were meeting. e) We didn't know where Karen was. We **hadn't seen** her all day.

3. a) When we arrived home, Dad **had cooked** the dinner. b) When my phone **rang**, I answered it. c) When Linda fell over, she **hurt** her knee. d) When he got to the shop, it **had closed**.

4. b) I went for a run as soon as it had stopped raining. c) Simon was late because he hadn't heard his alarm clock. d) I didn't see the post Justine had written.

7 Das *past progressive* (*The past progressive*)

Übungen ab S. 54

1. a) At 3 o'clock yesterday afternoon, Chris **was playing** his new computer game. b) Two years ago I **was living** in Berlin. c) Where **were** you **going** when I saw you on Saturday morning? d) At this time last week, we **were lying** on the beach in Spain. e) No, I **wasn't watching** TV! I **was doing** my homework! f) They **were waiting** for their teacher in Room 34, but the lesson was in Room 36. g) One year ago we **were starting** to learn French. h) Gina went home because she **wasn't feeling** well.

2. a) I was finishing my homework. b) She was wearing jeans and a T-shirt. c) I was meeting friends at the cinema. d) I was sleeping.

8 Das *simple past* und das *past progressive* (*The simple past and the past progressive*)

Übungen ab S. 55

1. a) Jane fell over because she was looking at her phone. b) Our team was losing when John scored a goal. c) When I saw Mark, he was talking to Pete's girlfriend. d) I was feeling hot, so I took off my jacket. e) We were waiting at the bus stop when it started to rain. f) Liam was skateboarding when he fell and broke his leg. g) While I was listening to the radio, I heard my favourite song. h) The cat caught a mouse while it was running through the grass. i) The children were shouting when the teacher came into the room.

2. It a) **was** a cold day in the middle of winter. An icy wind b) **was blowing** and snow c) **was starting** to fall. People d) **were hurrying** home to get inside, away from the cold air. Tom e) **was going** home, too. He f) **didn't want** to miss his favourite TV show. Suddenly he g) **heard** someone shout: "Stop that man! He's stolen my rucksack!" Tom h) **looked** around. A man i) **was running** towards him. He j) **was holding** a green rucksack.

3. a) I **was checking** my e-mails when I got a text from Claire. b) When I saw Mrs Miller at the train station, I **said** hello. c) Matt burnt his mouth while he **was drinking** very hot tea. d) I found some money when I **was walking** my dog in the park. e) Zoe was surprised when Lisa **sent** her a birthday card. f) When we got up that morning, the sun **was shining**.

4. a) When the lesson **ended**, the children **closed** their books. b) Sean **was doing** his homework when his computer **crashed**. c) The accident **happened** because Andy **was driving** too fast. d) When the accident **happened**, somebody **called** the police. e) I **didn't hear** you because I **was talking** on the phone. f) Pat **lost** a tooth when the ball **hit** his face.

Bedingungssätze (*Conditional clauses*)

1 Bedingungssätze Typ 1 (*Conditional clauses, type 1*)

●○○ 1. Ergänze die Sätze mit den richtigen Verbformen. → Lösung S. 72

a) If you ____________________ (open) this link,
you ____________________ (see) dancing cats.

b) If we ____________________ (not / leave) now,
we ____________________ (miss) our train.

c) You ____________________ (can / buy) some water
if you ____________________ (be) thirsty.

d) Dylan ____________________ (lend) you some money
if you ____________________ (ask) him.

e) If they ____________________ (not / listen) to their teacher,
they ____________________ (get) into trouble.

f) If your bike ____________________ (not / have) lights,
car drivers ____________________ (not / see) you.

●○○ 2. Bringe die Wörter in die richtige Reihenfolge, um sinnvolle Sätze zu bilden. → Lösung S. 72

a) buy / a / money / if / new / I'll / game / enough / have / I / computer

____

b) one / if / new / lose / a / your / phone / get / you / won't / you

____

c) feel / stays / she'll / if / tired / up / she / late

____

d) I'll / by / it / bike / doesn't / if / rain / go

____

●●○ 3. Wähle jeweils eine Aussage aus jedem Kasten und bilde daraus einen Bedingungssatz Typ 1.

→ Lösung S. 72

• ~~children are hungry~~	• I stay in bed
• you write down the new words	• be cold
• I don't feel well	• ~~we get a pizza~~
• you throw this ball	• be the champions
• they win this match	• remember them
• you don't wear a jacket	• dog catch it

a) *If the children are hungry, we'll get a pizza.*

b) ______

c) ______

d) ______

e) ______

f) ______

●●○ 4. Ergänze mit einem Verb in der richtigen Verbform – Achtung: Manchmal brauchst du eine Verneinung.

→ Lösung S. 72

ask • eat • go • make • meet • send • speak

a) If you ______ the message now, Frank won't get it in time.

b) Paula ______ out with us this evening if she has time.

c) Shh! You'll wake up the baby if you ______ so much noise!

d) Ron ______ that if there is meat in it. He's a vegetarian.

e) If you tell me what time your train arrives, I ______ you at the station.

f) I'm angry with Theresa. I ______ to her if I see her at the party.

g) Dad will give us some money if we ______ him for it.

2 Bedingungssätze Typ 2 (*Conditional clauses, type 2*)

●○○ 1. Kreuze die Verbform an, die am besten in die Lücke passt. → Lösung S. 72

a) If I ______ Justin Bieber, I'd take a selfie with him.

☐ would meet ☐ met

b) If Jenny spoke more slowly, I ______ her better.

☐ would understand ☐ understood

c) Paul ______ with us if he didn't need to finish his school project.

☐ had come ☐ would come

d) I'd be upset if you ______ that photo online.

☐ would post ☐ posted

e) They would visit Paris if they ______ French.

☐ could speak ☐ will speak

f) Tom ______ out with Ella if she asked him.

☐ went ☐ would go

●○○ 2. Bilde aus den angegebenen Wörtern Fragesätze mit den Verbformen von Bedingungssätzen Typ 2. → Lösung S. 72

a) you / do / lose / your phone?

What would you do if you lost your phone?

b) you / go / can / travel / anywhere / in the world?

Where ______________________________

c) you / do / school / closed / tomorrow?

____

d) you / win / trip to London / who / take / with you?

____

●●○ 3. Annie will ein Haustier haben, aber sie weiß noch nicht, welches. Sie überlegt, was sie mit verschiedenen Tieren machen könnte.

→ Lösung S. 72

a) dog: take it / walks

If I had a dog, I could take it for walks.

b) bird: teach it / talk

___

c) fish: watch it / swim

___

d) cat: it sit / on my knee

___

e) hamster: play with it / after school

___

f) rat: carry / in pocket / always

___

●○○ 4. Ergänze die Bedingungsätze Typ 2 mit dem richtigen Verb in der richtigen Form. → Lösung S. 72

be • find • finish • help • learn • move

a) You ____________________ your homework faster if you stopped playing computer games.

b) If you ____________________ a lot of money, would you take it to the police?

c) If I had time, I ____________________ to play the guitar.

d) They'd go to the concert if the tickets ____________________ cheaper.

e) We ____________________ to a bigger house if we had enough money.

f) This wouldn't take so long if you ____________________ me!

●●○ 5. Du gibst deinen Freunden gerne Ratschläge. Lies die Situationen und bilde Sätze mit „*If I were you ...*". → Lösung S. 73

a) Jim wants to get fit. (jogging)

If I were you, I'd go jogging every day.

b) Katie wants to learn a new language. (Spanish)

____

c) Chris wants to have a party while his parents are on holiday. (not / do that)

____

d) Cathy needs information for a school project. (search / online)

____

e) Amelie broke her mum's favourite vase. (not tell / anyone)

____

3 Bedingungssätze Typ 3 (*Conditional clauses, type 3*)

●○○ 1. Ergänze die Sätze mit den eingeklammerten Verben und verwende dabei die korrekte Form für Bedingungssätze Typ 3.

→ Lösung S. 73

a) If you ____________________ (go) to bed earlier,
you ____________________ (not / be) so tired all day.

b) We ____________________ (not miss) the train
if we ____________________ (leave) on time.

c) If he ____________________ (tell) the truth,
he ____________________ (not / get) into trouble.

d) I ____________________ (not / feel) so sick
if I ____________________ (not / eat) all that ice-cream!

e) If it ____________________ (snow) very heavily last night,
our school ____________________ (might / be) closed today.

●○○ 2. Ergänze die Bedingungssätze Typ 3 mit einem passenden Verb.

→ Lösung S. 73

drink • drive • know • read • not / ring

a) If you had listened to the teacher, you ____________________ the answer.

b) I might have enjoyed the film more if I ____________________ the book first.

c) If she ____________________ more water, she wouldn't have been so thirsty.

d) My mum ____________________ us to the station if we'd asked her.

e) If the postman ____________________ the doorbell, I wouldn't have woken up so early.

●○○ 3. Steht die Abkürzung "'d" für *would* oder für *had*?
Markiere jeweils die richtige Alternative. → Lösung S. 73

a) If I'd (*would* / *had*) had more time,
I'd (*would* / *had*) have helped you with your school project.

b) She'd (*would* / *had*) have come over to say hello
if she'd (*would* / *had*) seen us in the café.

c) We'd (*would* / *had*) have missed our flight
if we'd (*would* / *had*) left home later than 10 o'clock.

d) If they'd (*would* / *had*) been quiet,
they'd (*would* / *had*) have heard the teacher come into the room.

e) You'd (*would* / *had*) have stayed with me
if you'd (*would* / *had*) really loved me.

f) If I'd (*would* / *had*) got your message,
I'd (*would* / *had*) have known where to meet you.

●●○ 4. Finde und verbessere die Fehler in den Sätzen. → Lösung S. 73

a) I'd have lent you some money if you would have asked me.

____

b) The accident would have happened if Dave had been more careful.

____

c) It had have been a nice day if it hadn't rained.

____

d) I wouldn't have learned to speak French if I had lived in Paris
when I was young.

____

e) He could had become famous if more people had bought his CDs.

____

●●○ 5. Was wäre gewesen wenn … Schreibe in Form von Bedingungssätzen Typ 3, was in der vorgegebenen Situation anders gewesen wäre, wenn …

→ Lösung S. 73

a) We missed the start of the film because we were late.

If we hadn't been late, we ______________________

b) I met Jack when I went to Brighton on holiday.

____

c) Lucy was ill, so she didn't come out with us.

____

d) They weren't hungry, so they didn't eat lunch.

____

e) I couldn't call my parents because I forgot to take my phone.

____

f) Lucas went rock climbing and broke his leg.

____

●●○ 6. Vervollständige die Geschichte.

→ Lösung S. 74

Charlotte left her rucksack on the train last week.

a) not leave rucksack / train / not lose purse

If she hadn't left her rucksack on the train,

she wouldn't have lost her purse.

b) not lose purse / have enough money / for coffee

____

c) have enough money / for coffee / go to café

____

d) go to café / see boyfriend / with another girl

____

4 Bedingungssätze – Gemischte Aufgaben (*Conditional clauses – mixed forms*)

●○○ 1. Bedingungssatz Typ 1 (könnte passieren) oder Typ 2 (passiert eher unwahrscheinlich)? Markiere die beste Verbform.

→ Lösung S. 74

a) If I am / were head teacher of my school,
I will / would buy more computers for the library.

b) If Mum doesn't / didn't like her present,
I will / would take it back to the shop.

c) Where will / would you live
if you can / could choose anywhere in the world?

d) Tom will / would send you the link
if you give / gave him your e-mail address.

e) If you don't / didn't practise the guitar,
you won't / wouldn't be able to play well.

f) If we play / played loud music all night,
our neighbours will / would call the police.

●○○ 2. Bilde Bedingungssätze Typ 1 oder Typ 2.

→ Lösung S. 74

a) We're the best team. If we ______________________ (win),
we ______________________ (have) a big party.

b) We're the worst team. If we ______________________ (win),
we ______________________ (be) very surprised.

c) If I ______________________ (have) enough pocket money left,
I ______________________ (buy) that new game.

d) If I ______________________ (have) enough money,
I ______________________ (buy) a horse.

●●○ 3. Verbinde die Satzteile, die zusammenpassen. → Lösung S. 74

a) If I were you,	we'll send him a text.
b) I can't buy those shoes	if she has a party next weekend.
c) We'd miss you	I'd stay in bed all day.
d) If we need to contact him,	I wouldn't drink so much cola.
e) Would you tell me	if I don't understand the homework?
f) Jane will invite us	if they cost that much.
g) If our school was closed,	we'll leave without him.
h) Will you help me	if you went away.
i) If Max doesn't hurry up,	I'd call it Benjy.
j) If I had a dog,	if you didn't like my new hair-cut?

●●○ 4. Kreuze an, was in die Lücke gehört. → Lösung S. 74

a) If he'd switched on his phone, he ______ my message.
☐ would see ☐ would have seen

b) Granny would be very happy if you ______ her.
☐ had visited ☐ visited

c) If she had seen those photos, she ______ very angry!
☐ would be ☐ would have been

d) If you ______ a famous person to dinner, who would you invite?
☐ could have invited ☐ could invite

e) Emily wouldn't have fallen asleep if the film ______ more interesting.
☐ had been ☐ was

●●● 5. Schreibe Bedingungssätze, Typ 1, 2 oder 3, die zu diesen Situationen passen.

→ Lösung S. 74

a) You don't know what you have to do for history homework.

(text Josh / tell you)

If you text Josh, he ...

b) You would like to go to the cinema with your friends, but you don't have enough money. (had / go)

____

c) You and your friends wanted to go to the beach yesterday, but it rained all day. (rain / go)

____

d) You have got a present for Anna. You will probably see her later. (see / give)

____

●●● 6. Vervollständige die Bedingungssätze Typ 1, 2 oder 3.

→ Lösung S. 74

cost • do • feel • have • phone • remember • stay • visit

a) If we __________________ at a hotel on our last holiday, it __________________ too much money.

b) Harry isn't very fit. He __________________ better if he __________________ some sport.

c) I __________________ my grandpa this weekend if I __________________ .

d) If we __________________ friends in Berlin, we __________________ them in the school holidays.

1 Bedingungssätze Typ 1 (*Conditional clauses, type 1*)

→ Übungen ab S. 61

1. a) If you **open** this link, you **will see** dancing cats. b) If we **don't leave** now, we **will miss** our train. c) You **can buy** some water if you **are** thirsty. d) Dylan **will lend** you some money if you **ask** him. e) If they **don't listen** to their teacher, they **will get** in trouble. f) If your bike **doesn't have** lights, car drivers **won't see** you.

2. a) I'll buy a new computer game if I have enough money. b) If you lose your phone, you won't get a new one. c) She'll feel tired if she stays up late. d) I'll go by bike if it doesn't rain.

3. b) If you write down the new words, you'll remember them. c) If I don't feel well, I'll stay in bed. d) If you throw this ball, the dog will catch it. e) If they win this match, they'll be the champions. f) If you don't wear a jacket, you'll be cold.

4. a) If you **don't send** the message now, Frank won't get it in time. b) Paula **will go** out with us this evening if she has time. c) Shh! You'll wake up the baby if you **make** so much noise! d) Ron **won't eat** that if there is meat in it. He's a vegetarian. e) If you tell me what time your train arrives, I **will meet** you at the station. f) I'm angry with Theresa. I **won't speak** to her if I see her at the party. g) Dad will give us some money if we **ask** him for it.

2 Bedingungssätze Typ 2 (*Conditional clauses, type 2*)

→ Übungen ab S. 63

1. a) If I **met** Justin Bieber, I'd take a selfie with him. b) If Jenny spoke more slowly, I **would understand** her better. c) Paul **would come** with us if he didn't need to finish his school project. d) I'd be upset if you **posted** that photo online. e) They would visit Paris if they **could speak** French. f) Tom **would go** out with Ella if she asked him.

2. b) Where would you go if you could travel anywhere in the world? c) What would you do if your school was closed tomorrow? d) If you won a trip to London, who would you take with you?

3. b) If I had a bird, I could teach it to talk. c) If I had a fish, I could watch it swim. d) If I had a cat, it could sit on my knee. e) If I had a hamster, I could play with it after school. f) If I had a rat, I could always carry it around in my pocket.

4. a) You **would finish** your homework faster if you stopped playing computer games. b) If you **found** a lot of money, would you take it to the police? c) If I had time, I **would learn** to play the guitar. d) They'd go to the concert if the tickets **were** cheaper. e) We **would move** to a bigger house if we had enough money. f) This wouldn't take so long if you **helped** me!

5. b) If I were you, I'd learn Spanish. c) If I were you, I wouldn't do that. d) If I were you, I'd search for the information online. e) If I were you, I wouldn't tell anyone.

3 Bedingungssätze Typ 3 (*Conditional clauses, type 3*)

→ Übungen ab S. 66

1. a) If you **had gone** to bed earlier, you **wouldn't have been** so tired all day. b) We **wouldn't have missed** the train if we **had left** on time. c) If he **had told** the truth, he **wouldn't have got** into trouble. d) I **wouldn't have felt** so sick if I **hadn't eaten** all that ice-cream! e) If it **had snowed** very heavily last night, our school **might have been closed** today.

2. a) If you had listened to the teacher, you **would have known** the answer. b) I might have enjoyed the film more if I **had read** the book first. c) If she **had drunk** more water, she wouldn't have been so thirsty. d) My mum **would have driven** us to the station if we'd asked her. e) If the postman **hadn't rung** the doorbell, I wouldn't have woken up so early.

3. a) If I **had** had more time, I **would** have helped you with your school project. b) She **would** have come over to say hello if she **had** seen us in the café. c) We **would** have missed our flight if we **had** left home later than 10 o'clock. d) If they **had** been quiet, they **would** have heard the teacher come into the room. e) You **would** have stayed with me if you **had** really loved me. f) If I **had** got your message, I **would** have known where to meet you.

4. a) I'd have lent you some money if you **had asked** me. b) The accident **wouldn't** have happened if Dave had been more careful. c) It **would** have been a nice day if it hadn't rained. d) I **would** have learned to speak French if I had lived in Paris when I was young. e) He could **have** become famous if more people had bought his CDs.

5. a) If we hadn't been late, we wouldn't have missed the start of the film. b) If I hadn't gone to Brighton on holiday, I wouldn't have met Jack. c) If Lucy hadn't been ill, she'd have come out with us. d) If they had been hungry, they'd have eaten lunch. e) If I'd remembered / hadn't forgotten to take my phone, I could have called my parents. f) If Lucas hadn't gone rock climbing, he wouldn't have broken his leg.

6. b) If she hadn't lost her purse, she'd have had enough money for coffee. c) If she'd had enough money for coffee, she'd have gone to the café. d) If she'd gone to the café, she'd have seen her boyfriend with another girl.

4 Bedingungssätze – Gemischte Aufgaben (*Conditional clauses – mixed forms*)

Übungen ab S. 69

1. a) If I **were** head teacher of my school, I **would buy** more computers for the library. b) If Mum **doesn't like** her present, I **will take** it back to the shop. c) Where **would** you **live** if you **could choose** anywhere in the world? d) Tom **will send** you the link if you **give** him your e-mail address. e) If you **don't practise** the guitar, you **won't be able to** play well. f) If we **played** loud music all night, our neighbours **would call** the police.

2. a) We're the best team. If we **win**, we **will have** a big party. b) We're the worst team. If we **won**, we **would be** very surprised. c) If I **have** enough pocket money left, I **will buy** that new game. d) If I **had** enough money, I **would buy** a horse.

3. a) If I were you, I wouldn't drink so much cola. b) I can't buy those shoes if they cost that much. c) We'd miss you if you went away. d) If we need to contact him, we'll send him a text. e) Would you tell me if you didn't like my new hair-cut? f) Jane will invite us if she has a party next weekend. g) If our school was closed tomorrow, I'd stay in bed all day. h) Will you help me if I don't understand the homework? i) If Max doesn't hurry up, we'll leave without him. j) If I had a dog, I'd call it Benjy.

4. a) If he'd switched on his phone, he **would have seen** my message. b) Granny would be very happy if you **visited** her. c) If she had seen those photos, she **would have been** very angry! d) If you **could invite** a famous person to dinner, who would you invite? e) Emily wouldn't have fallen asleep if the film **had been** more interesting.

5. a) If you text Josh, he will tell you what to do. b) If I had enough money, I'd go to the cinema with my friends. c) If it hadn't rained all day, we'd have gone to the beach. d) If I see Anna later, I'll give her the present.

6. a) If we **had stayed** at a hotel on our last holiday, it **would have cost** too much money. b) Harry isn't very fit. He **would feel** better if he **did** some sport. c) I **will phone** my grandpa this weekend if I **remember**. d) If we **had** friends in Berlin, we **would visit** them in the school holidays.

Reflexivpronomen (*Reflexive pronouns*)

1 Reflexiver Gebrauch (*Reflexive use*)

●○○ 1. Füge das richtige Reflexivpronomen ein.
Du brauchst *myself*, *yourself*, *himself*, …

→ Lösung S. 83

a) Did you all enjoy ____________________ at Fiona's party?

b) Ouch! I've just cut ____________________ with this knife!

c) When my dad gets home from work, he always makes ____________________ a cup of coffee.

d) The dog hurt ____________________ when it fell into a hole.

e) The children wore helmets to protect ____________________ while they were riding their bikes.

f) Maria taught ____________________ to speak Italian.

g) We made ____________________ some sandwiches for lunch.

●○○ 2. Ergänze die Sätze mit dem richtigen Verb und Reflexivpronomen.

→ Lösung S. 83

buy • enjoy • hurt • look at • make • wash

a) Simon ____________________ in the mirror before he went out.

b) The holiday was terrible. We didn't ____________________ at all.

c) Be careful! If you fall, you might ____________________ !

d) I'm going to ____________________ a magazine to read on the train.

e) Hannah didn't have time for a shower, so she ____________________ quickly.

f) They sat down on the sofa and ____________________ comfortable.

●●○ 3. Brauchst du hier ein Reflexivpronomen oder nicht?
Wähle die richtige Alternative. → Lösung S. 83

a) We sat down on the beach and ______ .

☐ relaxed ourselves ☐ relaxed

b) How are you? Are you ______ better now?

☐ feeling ☐ feeling yourself

c) I'm busy at the moment. If you're thirsty, get ______ a drink.

☐ get yourselves ☐ get

d) I know we all went out that day, but I don't ______ what happened.

☐ remember ☐ remember myself

e) Did Louise ______ to play that song?

☐ teach herself ☐ teach

f) Wow – Joe looks different now! He has really ______ !

☐ changed ☐ changed himself

●●○ 4. Verbessere die Fehler, die du in diesen Sätzen findest. → Lösung S. 83

a) What time are we meeting ourselves this evening?

____

b) I hope Jack will hurry himself. We're going to be late.

____

c) I wonder myself if we will have a maths test tomorrow.

____

d) Imagine yourself if there were no more cars in our cities.

____

2 Verstärkender Gebrauch (*I can do it myself*)

●○○ 1. Beantworte die Fragen wie in dem Beispiel.
Verwende dabei Reflexivpronomen. → Lösung S. 83

a) Did someone help you make this cake?
(no / we / make)
No, we made it ourselves.

b) Can you help me with these exercises? (no / have to / do)

____

c) Who painted Susie's bedroom? (she / paint)

____

d) Did Tom's parents buy his new laptop for him? (no / buy)

____

e) Who broke your phone? (I / break)

____

●○○ 2. Vervollständige diesen Text
mit den richtigen Reflexivpronomen. → Lösung S. 83

Every year, there's a talent show at my school. Each class takes part, and the pupils have to organise everything a) ____________ . Last year, my class formed a band for the show. Elizabeth taught us a song she had written b) ____________ . Some people played instruments and some of us sang: we worked out the different parts c) ____________ . I was quite nervous but it was great fun! So why not try it d) ____________ and take part in this year's show with your friends?

●○○ 3. Verbinde die Sätze oder Satzteile, die zusammenpassen.

→ Lösung S. 83

a) I'm not going to clean your room.	the guitar herself.
b) Nobody wanted to eat his cake	all these exercises yourself?
c) We didn't have Halloween costumes	into the kitchen yourselves.
d) Nobody stole my phone.	Please clean it yourself.
e) Mary learnt to play	herself with her pocket money.
f) The pupils were allowed to	so he ate it himself.
g) Please take your dirty plates	my lunch myself.
h) Did you do	so we made them ourselves.
i) Marie bought the game	paint their classroom themselves.
j) I always make	I lost it myself.

●●○ 4. Übersetze die folgende Sätze ins Englische.

→ Lösung S. 84

a) Mache deine Hausaufgaben selbst.

___

b) Sie haben ihr neues Haus selbst gebaut.

___

c) Ben schrieb dieses Computer-Programm selbst.

___

d) Ja, wir haben die Fotos selbst gemacht.

___

e) Ich wasche meine Kleidung immer selbst.

___

3 *Each other*

●○○ 1. Schreibe Sätze darüber, was auf den Bildern zu sehen ist. Verwende dabei *each other*. → Lösung S. 84

a) They're ____________ (look)

b) ____________ (phone)

c) ____________ (play)

d) ____________ (give)

●○○ 2. Bringe die Wörter in die richtige Reihenfolge. → Lösung S. 84

a) known / other / we / for / years / have / each / five

____

b) other / kids / text / often / each / the

____

c) each / very / loved / Pat / other / much / Mary / and

____

●●○ 3. Vervollständige die Sätze mit dem richtigen Verb in der richtigen Form und ergänze each other.

→ Lösung S. 84

draw • help • not / like • not / love • see • send • not / speak • tell

a) Martin and Ruth had an argument. Now they ____________________ to ____________________ .

b) I would like you to work together and ____________________ with this project.

c) We always ____________________ cards at Christmas.

d) Chris and Marc aren't friends. They ____________________ .

e) Claire and I ____________________ every day at school.

f) In our last art lesson, we had to ____________________ pictures of ____________________ .

g) Her parents got divorced because they ____________________ any more.

h) We sat around the fire and ____________________ ghost stories.

●●○ 4. Schreibe einen zweiten Satz, der zum ersten passt, wie in dem Beispiel. Verwende dabei *each other*.

→ Lösung S. 84

a) Isabella and Lana are best friends. (really / like)

They really like each other.

b) Will you always remember me? (yes / we / never / forget)

____

c) I want to speak to you later. (let's / phone / evening)

____

d) We have no secrets. (tell / everything)

____

4 Gemischte Aufgaben (*Mixed forms*)

●○○ 1. Kreuze an, was in die Lücken passt. → Lösung S. 84

a) If you don't behave _________ , you will be in big trouble!

☐ yourselves ☐ each other

b) We talk to _________ on the phone nearly every day.

☐ ourselves ☐ each other

c) It's a great party! Are you all enjoying _________ ?

☐ yourselves ☐ each other

d) Luke and Jack sent _________ the photos they took.

☐ themselves ☐ each other

e) Please stop fighting, you two! You will hurt _________ !

☐ yourselves ☐ each other

f) Mum gave us some money to buy _________ something to eat.

☐ ourselves ☐ each other

●○○ 2. Brauchst du in diesen Sätzen ein Reflexivpronomen?
Wenn nicht, streiche es durch. → Lösung S. 84

a) I don't know where we are meeting ourselves this evening.

b) Did you make this yourself or did somebody help you?

c) Alex isn't feeling himself well today, so he's going to stay in bed.

d) She's really looking herself forward to her birthday!

e) Yes, I wrote this story myself. I hope you like it.

f) I couldn't sleep last night because I was worrying myself about the English test.

g) The cat hid itself behind the sofa.

●●○ 3. Füge ein Reflexivpronomen oder *each other* ein, wenn es nötig ist.

→ Lösung S. 84

a) Yesterday evening we relaxed ________________ on the sofa and watched TV.

b) I love my boyfriend and my boyfriend loves me. We think about ________________ all the time!

c) Imagine ________________ that you lost your key. What would you do?

d) Sally cleans ________________ her teeth three times a day.

e) My best friend and I usually give ________________ a nice birthday present.

f) "What happened to you?" "I cut ________________ while I was making a salad!"

g) They sat ________________ down in the classroom and waited for their teacher.

●●○ 4. Schreibe Sätze mit den Stichwörtern. Füge ein Reflexivpronomen oder *each other* ein, falls nötig.

→ Lösung S. 85

a) you / need / hurry / because / film / start / 10 minutes

____

b) they / always / send / interesting links

____

c) boys / not behave / on / school trip

____

d) you / remember / send Joanne / a text?

____

e) they / never talk / to

____

1 Reflexiver Gebrauch (*Reflexive use*)

→ Übungen ab S. 75

1. a) Did you all enjoy **yourselves** at Fiona's party? b) Ouch! I've just cut **myself** with this knife! c) When my dad gets home from work, he always makes **himself** a cup of coffee. d) The dog hurt **itself** when it fell into a hole. e) The children wore helmets to protect **themselves** while they were riding their bikes. f) Maria taught **herself** to speak Italian. g) We made **ourselves** some sandwiches for lunch.

2. a) Simon **looked at himself** in the mirror before he went out. b) The holiday was terrible. We didn't **enjoy ourselves** at all. c) Be careful! If you fall, you might **hurt yourself**! d) I'm going to **buy myself** a magazine to read on the train. e) Hannah didn't have time for a shower, so she **washed herself** quickly. f) They sat down on the sofa and **made themselves** comfortable.

3. a) We sat down on the beach and **relaxed**. b) How are you? Are you **feeling** better now? c) I'm busy at the moment. If you're thirsty, **get yourselves** a drink. d) I know we all went out that day but I don't **remember** what happened. e) Did Louise **teach herself** to play that song? f) Wow – Joe looks different now! He has really **changed**!

4. a) What time are we **meeting** this evening? b) I hope Jack will **hurry**. We're going to be late. c) I **wonder** if we will have a maths test tomorrow. d) **Imagine** if there were no more cars in our cities.

2 Verstärkender Gebrauch (*I can do it myself*)

→ Übungen ab S. 77

1. b) No, you have to do them yourself. c) She painted it herself. d) No, he bought it himself. e) I broke it myself.

2. Every year, there's a talent show at my school. Each class takes part, and the pupils have to organise everything a) **themselves**. Last year, my class formed a band for the show. Elizabeth taught us a song she had written b) **herself**. Some people played instruments and some of us sang: we worked out the different parts c) **ourselves**. I was quite nervous but it was great fun! So why not try it d) **yourself** and take part in this year's show with your friends?

3. a) I'm not going to clean your room. Please clean it yourself. b) Nobody wanted to eat his cake so he ate it himself. c) We didn't have Halloween costumes so we made them ourselves. d) Nobody stole my phone. I lost it myself. e) Mary learnt to play the guitar herself. f) The pupils were allowed to paint their classroom themselves. g) Please take your dirty plates into the kitchen yourselves. h) Did you do all these exercises yourself? i) Marie bought the game herself with her pocket money. j) I always make my lunch myself.

4. a) Do your homework yourself. b) They built their new house themselves. c) Ben wrote this computer program himself. d) Yes, we took the photos ourselves. e) I always wash my clothes myself.

3 *Each other*

Übungen ab S. 79

1. a) They're looking at each other. b) They're phoning each other. c) They're playing with each other. d) They're giving each other a present.

2. a) We have known each other for five years. b) The kids often text each other. c) Pat and Mary loved each other very much.

3. a) Martin and Ruth had an argument. Now they **aren't speaking** to **each other**. b) I would like you to work together and **help each other** with this project. c) We always **send each other** cards at Christmas. d) Chris and Marc aren't friends. They **don't like each other**. e) Claire and I **see each other** every day at school. f) In our last art lesson, we had to **draw** pictures of **each other**. g) Her parents got divorced because they **didn't love each other** anymore. h) We sat around the fire and **told each other** ghost stories.

4. b) Yes, we will never forget each other. c) Let's phone each other this evening. d) We tell each other everything.

4 Gemischte Aufgaben (*Mixed forms*)

Übungen ab S. 81

1. a) If you don't behave **yourselves**, you will be in big trouble! b) We talk to **each other** on the phone nearly every day. c) It's a great party! are you all enjoying **yourselves**? d) Luke and Jack sent **each other** the photos they took. e) Please stop fighting, you two! You will hurt **each other**! f) Mum gave us some money to buy **ourselves** something to eat.

2. a) I don't know where we are meeting ~~ourselves~~ this evening. b) Did you make this yourself or did somebody help you? c) Alex isn't feeling ~~himself~~ well today, so he's going to stay in bed. d) She's really looking ~~herself~~ forward to her birthday! e) Yes, I wrote this story myself. I hope you like it. f) I couldn't sleep last night because I was worrying ~~myself~~ about the English test. g) The cat hid ~~itself~~ behind the sofa.

3. a) Yesterday evening we **relaxed** on the sofa and watched TV. b) I love my boyfriend and my boyfriend loves me. We think about **each other** all the time! c) **Imagine** that you lost your key. What would you do? d) Sally **cleans** her teeth three times a day. e) My best friend and I usually give **each other** a nice birthday present. f) "What happened to you?" "I cut **myself** while I was making a salad!" g) They **sat down** in the classroom and waited for their teacher.

4. a) You need to hurry because the film starts in 10 minutes. b) They always send each other interesting links. c) The boys didn't behave themselves on the school trip. d) Did you remember to send Joanne a text? e) They never talk to each other.

Modalverben und ihre Ersatzverben (*Modals and their substitutes*)

1 Können: *can* – (*to*) *be able to*

●○○ 1. Deine Klasse fährt nächste Woche ins Schullandheim.
Schreibe Sätze mit *will / won't be able to*. → Lösung S. 94

a) We ______________________________ (take)

b) We ______________________________ (swim)

c) We ______________________________ (play)

d) We ______________________________ (sleep / late)

●○○ 2. Schreibe diese Sätze in der Vergangenheit. → Lösung S. 94

a) Ron can swim.

Ron ______________ when he was six years old.

b) They can speak Spanish.

They ______________ three years ago.

c) We can't help you.

______________________________ yesterday.

d) I can't hear the teacher.

I ______________ the teacher during the history lesson.

●○○ 3. Wähle die Zeitform, die in den Sätzen passt. → Lösung S. 94

a) School finishes at 1 o'clock, so we'll have been able / we'll be able to meet at 1.30.

b) We were able to / have been able to go on a boat trip while we were in London.

c) He won't be able to / hasn't been able to sleep well all this week.

d) I haven't been able to / wasn't able to finish my homework yesterday.

e) Will you be able to / Have you been able to come with us next Saturday?

f) They haven't been able to / weren't able to see that film yet.

●●○ 4. Füge eine Form von *be able to* und das richtige Verb ein. Überlege dabei, ob du das *will future*, *simple past* oder *present perfect* brauchst. → Lösung S. 94

come • do • find • meet • play • see • take • tell

a) Sorry, we ____________________ to your party next week.

b) ______________ you ____________________ Tony yet? I really need to speak to him.

c) You ____________________ the whole city centre when we climb to the top of the tower.

d) I saw the accident, so I ____________________ the police what happened.

e) My camera has been broken all week. I ____________________ any photos.

f) Yes, they ____________________ me at the station yesterday.

g) Judy ____________________ the guitar since she was nine.

h) It was a difficult exercise. Nobody ____________________ it.

2 Dürfen, nicht dürfen: *can – may – mustn't – (to) be allowed to*

●○○ 1. Was fragst du in der gegebenen Situation? Überlege, ob der Ton neutral (*can*) oder höflich (*may*) sein soll. → Lösung S. 94

a) You need a pen but you don't have one. (borrow)

Can I borrow your pen?

b) You have finished your meal in a café and want to pay. (have / bill)

____

c) You need 10 euros for a school trip. (give)

____

d) You are bored at your aunt's house and want to leave. (go home)

____

e) You want your teacher to explain something. (ask / question)

____

f) You call your friend and her dad answers the phone. (speak / Marie)

____

●○○ 2. Ergänze die Sätze mit *can* oder *mustn't*. → Lösung S. 94

a) We ________________ talk while we are doing a test at school.

b) At our school, we ________________ eat in the cafeteria or bring our own sandwiches.

c) You ________________ work on this project with a partner if you want to.

d) The pupils ________________ use their phones in the classroom.

e) You ________________ run in the corridor. Walk, please!

f) I ____________ do this homework at the weekend, but I ________________ forget to take it to school on Monday!

●○○ 3. Schreibe in ganzen Sätzen, was Paula vor drei Jahren durfte / nicht durfte und was sie in fünf Jahren darf / nicht darf. → Lösung S. 94

Paula	3 years ago	in 5 years
stay up until 11 p.m.	✗	✓
travel for free on the bus	✓	✗
learn to drive	✗	✓
have a dog	✓	✗

a) *Paula wasn't allowed to stay up until 11 p.m. 3 years ago.*

b) ____

c) ____

d) ____

e) ____

f) ____

g) ____

h) ____

●●○ 4. Ergänze *be allowed to* in der richtigen Zeitform. Aufpassen: der Satz kann auch eine negative Form verlangen. → Lösung S. 95

a) The tour of the zoo was great! We ________________ feed some of the animals!

b) The test hasn't finished. The pupils ________________ leave the room yet.

c) Please listen to the story without talking. You ________________ to ask questions at the end.

d) ________ we ________________ watch the film tomorrow evening?

e) "Was James at the party?" "No, he ________________ to come."

f) Lena ________________ do her homework late this week.

3 Müssen / nicht brauchen: *must* – (*to*) *have to* – *needn't*

●○○ 1. Ergänze mit *must* oder *needn't*. → Lösung S. 95

a) If you don't like this pasta, you ________________ eat it.

b) We ________________ walk. We can take the bus.

c) Mike needs this information today. I ________________ send it to him now.

d) You ________________ explain the exercise to me – I understand it.

e) I can't come out with you this evening. I ________________ do some revision for the geography test.

f) We ________________ bring the money tomorrow. We can bring it next week.

●○○ 2. Ändere die Zeitform wie in dem Beispiel.
Überlege auch, ob weitere Änderungen nötig sind. → Lösung S. 95

a) We must be at the theatre at 7 o'clock. (tomorrow)

We will have to be at the theatre at 7 o'clock tomorrow.

b) I must buy some new shoes before my holiday. (last month)

____

c) Lisa needn't go to basketball ball training today. (next Saturday)

____

d) Peter needn't get up early this week. (last week)

____

e) They must learn a lot of new vocabulary. (this week)

____

f) I needn't download new software. (this month)

____

●●○ 3. Welche Sätze aus dem unteren Kasten passen zu den oberen?

→ Lösung S. 95

a) The roads are very wet today.
b) Harry arrived on time.
c) We're not having the history test tomorrow.
d) Julia's dog ate her homework.
e) There isn't anything to eat because I didn't go shopping.

1 That's great! Now I won't have to study this evening!
2 She had to do it all again.
3 You'll have to be careful on your bike.
4 We'll have to order a pizza for dinner.
5 We didn't have to wait for him.

a) ______ b) ______ c) ______ d) ______ e) ______

●●○ 4. Ergänze mit dem richtigen Verb in der richtigen Zeitform von *must* oder *needn't*.

→ Lösung S. 95

be • buy • walk • wear

a) I won't be here this afternoon, so someone ____________________ the dog for me.

b) We ____________________ any more milk. We had enough for the weekend.

c) It's going to be hot later today. You ____________________ a jacket.

d) We ____________________ quiet because the class in the next room was taking a test.

4 Gemischte Aufgaben (*Mixed forms*)

1. Kreuze an, was am besten passt. → Lösung S. 95

a) My bike is broken. I ______ ride it this week.

☐ won't be able to ☐ won't be allowed to

b) We looked everywhere, but we ______ find the key.

☐ weren't able to ☐ weren't allowed to

c) After they'd finished their homework, the children ______ watch TV.

☐ were able to ☐ were allowed to

d) There has been a lot of noise in our street this week.

We ______ sleep well.

☐ haven't been able to ☐ haven't been allowed to

e) Because it's so cold, my cat ______ sleep on my bed this week.

☐ has been able to ☐ has been allowed to

2. Positiv oder negativ? Schreibe die Form, die Sinn macht.
Denke dabei auch an die richtige Zeitform. → Lösung S. 95

a) She ______________________ (have to) learn the new vocabulary because she already knew all the words.

b) No, we ______________________ (be allowed to) use a dictionary in the test tomorrow.

c) Josie ______________________ (be able to) take us sightseeing when we visit her.

d) We ______________________ (have to) take our passports when we fly to England next summer.

●●○ 3. Erzähle, was deine Mutter in ihrer Kindheit tun durfte und was sie nicht durfte.

→ Lösung S. 96

- Go to bed: 7.30 p.m.
- No TV during the week
- Extra homework at the weekend
- Can't phone friends during the week
- Help her mum clean and cook
- No shopping with friends

a) *She had to go to bed at 7.30 p.m.*

b) ____________________

c) ____________________

d) ____________________

e) ____________________

f) ____________________

●●○ 4. Ergänze die Sätze mit *be able to, be allowed to* oder *have to* in der richtigen Zeitform.

→ Lösung S. 96

a) I hope David ____________ come to the concert with us, but he has to ask his parents first.

b) The last bus had left, so we ____________ take a taxi from the station.

c) I'm sorry I ____________ call you. I didn't have time.

d) It's OK: they speak English at the hotel. We ____________ speak Italian.

e) The children ____________ play computer games all day. They had to play outside, too.

1 Können:
can – (to) be able to

Übungen ab S. 86

1. a) We won't be able to take our phones. b) We'll be able to swim. c) We'll be able to play table tennis. d) We won't be able to sleep late.

2. a) Ron **was able to swim** when he was six years old. b) They **were able to speak Spanish** three years ago. c) We **weren't able to help you** yesterday. d) I **wasn't able to hear** the teacher during the history lesson.

3. a) School finishes at 1 o'clock, so **we'll be able to** meet at 1.30. b) We **were able to** go on a boat trip while we were in London. c) He **hasn't been able to** sleep well all this week. d) I **wasn't able to** finish my homework yesterday. e) **Will you be able to** come with us next Saturday? f) They **haven't been able to** see that film yet.

4. a) Sorry, we **won't be able to come** to your party next week. b) **Have** you **been able to find** Tony yet? I really need to speak to him. c) You **will be able to see** the whole city centre when we climb to the top of the tower. d) I saw the accident, so I **was able to tell** the police what happened. e) My camera has been broken all week. I **haven't been able to take** any photos. f) Yes, they **were able to meet** me at the station yesterday. g) Judy **has been able to play** the guitar since she was nine. h) It was a difficult exercise. Nobody **was able to do** it.

2 Dürfen, nicht dürfen:
can – may – mustn't – (to) be allowed to

Übungen ab S. 88

1. b) May I have the bill, please? c) Can you give me 10 euros for the school trip? d) Can we go home now? e) May I ask you a question? f) May I speak to Marie, please?

2. a) We **mustn't talk** while we are doing a test at school. b) At our school, we **can** eat in the cafeteria or bring our own sandwiches. c) You **can** work on this project with a partner if you want to. d) The pupils **mustn't** use their phones in the classroom. e) You **mustn't** run in the corridor. Walk, please! f) I **can** do this homework at the weekend, but I **mustn't** forget to take it to school on Monday!

3. b) Paula **will be allowed to** stay up until 11 p.m. in 5 years. c) Paula **was allowed to** travel for free on the bus 3 years ago. d) Paula **won't be allowed to** travel for free on the bus in 5 years. e) Paula **wasn't allowed to** learn to drive 3 years ago. f) Paula **will be allowed to** learn to drive in 5 years. g) Paula **was allowed to** have a dog 3 years ago. h) Paula **won't be allowed to** have a dog in 5 years.

4. a) The tour of the zoo was great! We **were allowed to** feed some of the animals! b) The test hasn't finished. The pupils **haven't been allowed to** leave the room yet. c) Please listen to the story without talking. You **will be allowed to** task questions at the end. d) **Will** we **be allowed to** watch the film tomorrow evening? e) "Was James at the party?" "No, he **wasn't allowed to** come." f) Lena **has been allowed to** do her homework late this week.

3 Müssen/nicht brauchen: *must – (to) have to – needn't*

→ Übungen ab S. 90

1. a) If you don't like this pasta, you **needn't** eat it. b) We **needn't** walk. We can take the bus. c) Mike needs this information today. I **must** send it to him now. d) You **needn't** explain the exercise to me – I understand it. e) I can't come out with you this evening. I **must** do some revision for the geography test. f) We **needn't** bring the money tomorrow. We can bring it next week.

2. b) I **had to** buy some new shoes before my holiday last month. c) Lisa **won't have to go** to basketball training next Saturday. d) Peter **didn't have to** get up early last week. e) They **have had to** learn a lot of new vocabulary this week. f) I **haven't had to** download new software this month.

3. a) The roads are very wet today. (3) You'll have to be careful on your bike. b) Harry arrived on time. (5) We didn't have to wait for him. c) We're not having the history test tomorrow. (1) That's great! Now I won't have to study this evening! d) Julia's dog ate her homework. (2) She had to do it all again. e) There isn't anything to eat because I didn't go shopping. (4) We'll have to order a pizza for dinner.

4. a) I won't be here this afternoon, so someone **will have to walk** the dog for me. b) We **didn't have to buy** any more milk. We had enough for the weekend. c) It's going to be hot later today. You **won't need to wear** a jacket. d) We **had to be** quiet because the class in the next room was taking a test.

4 Gemischte Aufgaben (*Mixed forms*)

→ Übungen ab S. 92

1. a) My bike is broken. I **won't be able to** ride it this week. b) We looked everywhere, but we **weren't able to** find the key. c) After they'd finished their homework, the children **were allowed to** watch TV. d) There has been a lot of noise in our street this week. We **haven't been able to** sleep well. e) Because it's so cold, my cat **has been allowed to** sleep on my bed this week.

2. a) She **didn't have to** learn the new vocabulary because she already knew all the words. b) No, we **won't be allowed to** use a dictionary in the test tomorrow. c) Josie **will be able to** take us sightseeing when we visit her. d) We **will have to** take our passports when we fly to England next summer.

3. b) She wasn't allowed to watch TV during the week. c) She had to do extra homework at the weekend. d) She wasn't allowed to phone her friends during the week. e) She had to help her mum clean and cook. f) She wasn't allowed to go shopping with her friends.

4. a) I hope David **will be allowed to** come to the concert with us, but he has to ask his parents first. b) The last bus had left, so we **had to** take a taxi from the station. c) I'm sorry I **wasn't able to** call you. I didn't have time. d) It's OK: they speak English at the hotel. We **won't have** to speak Italian. e) The children **weren't allowed to** play computer games all day. They had to play outside, too.

Besondere Formen des Adjektivs (*Special forms of adjectives*)

1 Das Adjektiv als Nomen (*Adjectives as nouns*)

●○○ 1. Schreibe die Sätze um, indem du die unterstrichenen Wörter wie in dem Beispiel veränderst. → Lösung S. 102

a) It can be difficult for young people to find a job.

It can be difficult for the young to find a job.

b) We should do more to help poor people.

____

c) I like reading online magazines about people who are famous.

____

d) People who are rich often have expensive cars.

____

e) There are some special computer programs for blind people.

____

●○○ 2. Fülle die Lücken indem du aus den angegebenen Adjektiven ein Nomen machst. → Lösung S. 102

disabled • famous • poor • rich • sick • young

a) In many countries, the ____________ have to live on the streets.

b) I work in a hospital because I want to help the ____________ .

c) The ____________ often travel first class.

d) The ____________ never write letters – they just text their friends.

e) A lot of people like to take selfies with the ____________ .

f) Chris spent a year working with ____________ after he left school.

●○○ 3. Kreuze die beste Lösung an. → Lösung S. 102

a) Paul's a celebrity photographer. He takes pictures of ______ .

☐ the old ☐ the famous ☐ the young

b) Guide dogs are trained to help ______ , for example by helping them to walk along the street safely.

☐ the blind ☐ the rich ☐ the poor

c) It is not always easy for ______ to travel by train or bus, especially if they are in a wheelchair.

☐ the rich ☐ the young ☐ the disabled

d) After the accident, the police spoke to the families of ______ .

☐ the famous ☐ the dead ☐ the blind

e) It is very sad for ______ if they have nobody to talk to.

☐ the old ☐ the rich ☐ the dead

f) At Christmas, a lot of people give money to help ______ .

☐ the young ☐ the famous ☐ the poor

g) ______ don't understand what it feels like to have no money for food.

☐ the blind ☐ the rich ☐ the old

●○○ 4. Was passt: *the* + *adjective* oder *adjective* + *noun*? → Lösung S. 102

a) He helped the blind / the blind man to cross the road.

b) Many people believe the rich / a rich person should do more to help others.

c) At first, they didn't know who the dead / the dead woman was.

d) This organisation collects food and toys for the poor / the poor girl.

e) We are glad that the sick / the sick children are almost better now.

2 Adjektive nach bestimmten Verben (*Adjectives after certain verbs*)

●○○ 1. Ergänze die Sätze mit einem passenden Adjektiv. → Lösung S. 102

bad • beautiful • boring • calm • excited • famous • friendly • good • hungry • tired

a) It was Christmas Eve and the children were ________________ .

b) You might get ________________ later, so take a sandwich with you.

c) I don't want to see that film – it sounds really ________________ .

d) My sister looked ________________ in her wedding dress.

e) Jack became ________________ when his first song was a hit.

f) I thought the soup would taste ________________ , but it was too salty.

g) We felt ________________ because we had been walking all day.

h) The dog seemed ________________ , but then it started to bark at us.

i) If the milk smells ________________ , don't drink it!

j) It is important to stay ________________ if there is a fire in the building.

●○○ 2. Notiere dir hier die besonderen Adjektivkonstruktionen mit dem Verb aus Übung 1 noch einmal. → Lösung S. 102

a) *to be excited* b) ________________

c) ________________ d) ________________

e) ________________ f) ________________

g) ________________ h) ________________

i) ________________ j) ________________

●○○ 3. Finde zu jedem Bild ein passendes Verb mit Adjektiv. → Lösung S. 102

feel | look | smell | taste | be | get

good | expensive | angry | cold | happy | good

a) *He* ____________________

____

b) *The flowers* ____________________

____

c) *She* ____________________

____

d) *The milk doesn't* ____________________

____

e) *The car* ____________________

____

f) *The bear* ____________________

____

●○○ 4. Verbinde die Satzteile, die zusammenpassen. → Lösung S. 103

a) It's getting	wear your hat and stay warm!
b) Joanna seems busy now,	interesting – I really want to read it.
c) That book sounds	She got 100 % in the maths test.
d) These shoes feel really	dark – please come inside now.
e) Jenny's dream is to become	Where did you take them?
f) Most children like ice-cream	rich and buy a villa in France.
g) It's very cold today –	terrible! Please open the window!
h) Marie is clever.	so I'll talk to her later.
i) This room smells	because it tastes sweet.
j) The photos look great!	uncomfortable. I can't wear them.

●○○ 5. Wähle eine passende Kombination von Verb und Adjektiv. → Lösung S. 103

a) The coffee ______ .

☐ smelled beautiful ☐ tasted bitter

b) When I had a problem, my teacher ______ .

☐ was helpful ☐ sounded happy

c) Dad ______ when we told him about the broken window.

☐ became angry ☐ looked interested

d) The weather ______ for two months last winter.

☐ felt nice ☐ stayed cold

e) The party ______ , so we didn't go.

☐ got hot ☐ sounded boring

f) If you ______ , take a short break.

☐ feel tired ☐ seem busy

1 Das Adjektiv als Nomen (*Adjectives as nouns*)

Übungen ab S. 97

1. b) We should do more to help **the poor**. c) I like reading online magazines about **the famous**. d) **The rich** often have expensive cars. e) There are some special computer programs for **the blind**.

2. a) In many countries, the **poor** have to live on the streets. b) I work in a hospital because I want to help the **sick**. c) The **rich** often travel first class. d) The **young** never write letters – they just text their friends. e) A lot of people like to take selfies with the **famous**. f) Chris spent a year working with the **disabled** after he left school.

3. a) Paul's a celebrity photographer. He takes pictures of **the famous**. b) Guide dogs are trained to help **the blind**, for example by helping them to walk along the street safely. c) It is not always easy for **the disabled** to travel by train or bus, especially if they are in a wheelchair. d) After the accident, the police spoke to the families of **the dead**. e) It is very sad for **the old** if they have nobody to talk to. f) At Christmas, a lot of people give money to help **the poor**. g) **The rich** don't understand what it feels like to have no money for food.

4. a) He helped **the blind man** to cross the road. b) Many people believe that **the rich** should do more to help others. c) At first, they didn't know who **the dead woman** was. d) This organisation collects food and toys for **the poor**. e) We are glad that **the sick children** are almost better now.

2 Adjektive nach bestimmten Verben (*Adjectives after certain verbs*)

Übungen ab S. 99

1. a) It was Christmas Eve and the children were **excited**. b) You might get **hungry** later, so take a sandwich with you. c) I don't want to see that film – it sounds really **boring**. d) My sister looked **beautiful** in her wedding dress. e) Jack became **famous** when his first song was a hit. f) I thought the soup would taste **good**, but it was too salty. g) We felt **tired** because we had been walking all day. h) The dog seemed **friendly**, but then it started to bark at us. i) If the milk smells **bad**, don't drink it! j) It is important to stay **calm** if there is a fire in the building.

2. a) to be excited b) to get hungry c) to sound boring d) to look beautiful e) to become famous f) to taste good g) to feel tired h) to seem friendly i) to smell bad j) to stay calm

3. a) He **looks cold**. b) The flowers **smell good**. c) She **feels happy**. d) The milk doesn't **taste good**. e) The car **is expensive**. f) The bear **got angry**.

4. a) It's getting dark – please come inside now. b) Joanna seems busy now, so I'll take to her later. c) That book sounds interesting – I really want to read it! d) These shoes feel really uncomfortable. I can't wear them. e) Jenny's dream is to become rich and buy a villa in France. f) Most children like ice-cream because it tastes sweet. g) It's very cold today – wear your hat and stay warm! h) Marie is clever. She got 100 % in the maths test. i) This room smells terrible! Please open the window! j) The photos look great! Where did you take them?

5. a) The coffee **tasted bitter**. b) When I had a problem, my teacher **was helpful**. c) Dad **became angry** when we told him about the broken window. d) The weather **stayed cold** for two months last winter. e) The party **sounded boring**, so we didn't go. f) If you **feel tired**, take a short break.

Der bestimmte und der unbestimmte Artikel (*The definite and indefinite article*)

1 Der bestimmte Artikel (*The definite article*)

●○○ 1. Bilde aus den Stichwörtern ganze Sätze.
Füge einen bestimmten Artikel ein, falls nötig. → Lösung S. 106

a) when / next bus / leave?

___

b) they / play / music / in / that supermarket

c) school / is / opposite / library

___

d) Louise / not go / church

___

●●○ 2. Wie sagt man das auf Englisch? Übersetze. → Lösung S. 106

a) Emma geht jetzt zur Arbeit.

___

b) Mir gefällt die Musik nicht, die sie spielen.

___

c) Der 9 Uhr-Zug ist ziemlich langsam.

___

d) Sollen wir mit dem Zug fahren?

___

e) Das Abendessen ist fertig!

___

2 Der unbestimmte Artikel (*The indefinite article*)

●○○ 1. Füge das richtige Wort ein mit dem richtigen unbestimmten Artikel (*a* oder *an*) dazu. → Lösung S. 106

athlete • astronaut • aunt • dentist • headache • hurry • instrument • pupil • teacher • temperature

a) Please be quiet! I've got ____________.

b) My sister has just had a baby. That means I'm ____________ now!

c) Mrs Connolly is ____________ . She works at our school.

d) I can't stop now. I'm in ____________ .

e) Sam is interested in teeth. He wants to be ____________ when he leaves school.

f) She doesn't feel well and she's got ____________ .

g) Usain Bolt is ____________ . He's won a lot of gold medals.

h) I play the guitar. Can you play ____________ ?

i) Jerry still goes to school. He's ____________ at St Michael's.

j) Pete once met a man who is ____________ .

●●○ 2. Füge einen unbestimmten Artikel ein, wo es nötig ist. → Lösung S. 106

a) Mr Trent is ____________ maths teacher.

b) What kind of ____________ teacher is Mr Connor?

c) John became ____________ father last year when his son was born.

d) Does your little brother believe in ____________ Father Christmas?

e) Jenny is ____________ doctor and her sister is ____________ painter.

f) "____________ Doctor Who" is a popular television programme.

1 Der bestimmte Artikel (*The definite article*)

→ Übungen ab S. 106

1. a) When does **the** next bus leave? b) They play music in that supermarket. c) **The** school is opposite **the** library. d) Louise doesn't go to church.

2. a) Emma is going to work now. b) I don't like the music that they're playing. c) The 9 o'clock train is quite slow. d) Shall we go by train? e) Dinner is ready!

2 Der unbestimmte Artikel (*The indefinite article*)

→ Übungen ab S. 105

1. a) Please be quiet! I've got **a headache**. b) My sister has just had a baby. That means I'm **an aunt** now! c) Mrs Connolly is **a teacher**. She works at our school. d) I can't stop now. I'm in **a hurry**. e) Sam is interested in teeth. He wants to be **a dentist** when he leaves school. f) She doesn't feel well and she's got **a temperature**. g) Usain Bolt is **an athlete**. He's won a lot of gold medals. h) I play the guitar. Can you play **an instrument**? i) Jerry still goes to school. He's a pupil at St Michael's. j) Pete once met a man who is **an astronaut**.

2. a) Mr Trent is **a** maths teacher. b) What kind of teacher is Mr Connor? c) John became **a** father last year when his son was born. d) Does your little brother believe in Father Christmas? e) Jenny is **a** doctor and her sister is **a** painter. f) "Doctor Who" is a popular television programme.

Paarwörter (*Pair words*)

1 Paarwörter (*Pair words*)

●○○ 1. Schreibe die Paarwörter auf, die zu den Bildern passen. → Lösung S. 108

a) She was wearing her new

__________________ at the party.

b) Do you like my new

__________________ ?

c) The kids wear __________________

when it's hot.

d) My grandma can't

read without her

__________________ .

●○○ 2. Wähle jeweils die beste Alternative in diesen Sätzen. → Lösung S. 108

a) Do you really need another jeans / pair of jeans?

b) I always wear pyjamas / a pyjama in bed when it's cold.

c) If you can't see the words on the blackboard, you might need a glasses / glasses.

d) I want a new pair of sunglasses / a new sunglasses. These ones are very old.

e) Tim often wears shorts / a short, even in winter!

1 Paarwörter (*Pair words*)

→ Übungen ab S. 107

1. a) She was wearing her new **trousers / jeans** at the party. b) Do you like my new **sunglasses**? c) The kids wear **shorts** when it's hot. d) My grandma can't read without her **glasses**.

2. a) Do you really need another **pair of jeans**? b) I always wear **pyjamas** in bed when it's cold. c) If you can't see the words on the blackboard, you might need **glasses**. d) I want **a new pair of sunglasses**. These ones are very old. e) Tim often wears **shorts**, even in winter!

Die indirekte Rede (*Indirect speech*)

1 Direkte und indirekte Rede (*Direct and indirect speech*)

●○○ 1. Ergänze Satzzeichen, damit die Sätze in der direkten Rede stehen.

→ Lösung S. 121

a) the - bus - leaves - in - 10 - minutes - said - Sophie

"The bus leaves in 10 minutes," said Sophie.

b) what - time - does - the - film - start - asked - Gracie

____

c) I - have - never - been - to - Italy - said - Paul

____

d) have - you - seen - my - keys - asked - Janie

____

e) there - will - be - a - German - test - tomorrow - said - Mrs Braun

____

●○○ 2. Schreibe die angegebenen Sätze in die direkte Rede um. Denke auch an die Satzzeichen.

→ Lösung S. 121

a) Claire told you that she's getting a dog next week.

________________________________ said Claire.

b) Harry said he's got a new girlfriend.

____

c) Jonas asked if he can borrow 5 euros.

____

●○○ 3. Welches Verb passt am besten? → Lösung S. 121

added • answered • explained • promised • said • told • wanted to know

a) Caroline ________________ that she would be home late that evening.

b) Mr Connors ________________ us this is really good website for practising English grammar.

c) Lara ________________ that she wouldn't tell my parents about the broken vase.

d) Mrs Summers ________________ that the cafeteria was downstairs, opposite the secretary's office.

e) He thanked us for coming and ________________ that it had been nice to meet us.

f) We asked if she wanted to come with us, but she ________________ that she didn't have time.

g) He ________________ what time the film started.

●●○ 4. Du triffst einen alten Freund, der dir Neuigkeiten aus seinem Leben erzählt. Berichte, was er dir gesagt hat. → Lösung S. 121

a) My brother works in a bank. (a supermarket)

He told me his brother …

b) My old dog died last year.

____

c) I'm going to university in September.

____

d) I don't live in Elder Street now.

____

2 Veränderung der Zeitform (*Tense change*)

●○○ 1. Schreibe die Sätze in die indirekte Rede um. → Lösung S. 121

a) "We're hungry!" said the children.

The children ______________________________

b) "I don't think it's a good idea," said Christina.

____

c) "I'll call you later," promised Joanna.

____

d) "Ted won't like this photo," Caroline told me.

____

e) "I don't want to talk to you!" said Richard.

____

f) "We're having a really great holiday!" said Dawn.

____

●○○ 2. Wähle die richtige Zeitform für die indirekte Rede. → Lösung S. 121

a) "I lived in China for three years."
He said he lived / had lived in China for three years.

b) "Angela didn't give me your message."
She explained that Angela hadn't given / didn't give her my message.

c) "No, I haven't cleaned my room yet."
She said she didn't clean / hadn't cleaned her room yet.

d) "Someone has eaten all the cookies!"
He said someone had eaten / ate all the cookies.

●○○ 3. Lies die Aussagen, die Sam über sich macht und schreibe sie in indirekter Rede auf.

→ Lösung S. 121

a) "I've got three cats."

d) "I had never been to the USA before."

b) "I can play the violin."

e) "I've met lots of famous people."

c) "I went to Florida last year."

f) "I'm having a big party on my next birthday."

a) Sam said ____________________

b) ____________________

c) ____________________

d) ____________________

e) ____________________

f) ____________________

●●○ 4. Ist die Zeitform in der indirekten Rede richtig?
Falls nicht, verbessere den Satz. → Lösung S. 121

a) "I sent Andy a lot of texts."
She said she sent Andy a lot of texts.

____

b) "I had never eaten sushi before."
He told us he had never eaten sushi before.

____

c) "It will be very cold tomorrow."
She said it had been very cold the next day.

____

d) "Max is going to meet us at half past six."
You told me Max was going to meet us at half past six.

____

e) "We have been waiting for a long time."
She said they were waiting for a long time.

____

●●○ 5. Schreibe die Sätze in die direkte Rede um. → Lösung S. 121

a) Robbie said he was very popular with his fans.

____

b) Susie told us she wasn't allowed to drink coffee.

____

c) Angie told me she was coming to my party.

____

d) Tom said he hadn't studied for the test.

____

3 Die indirekte Rede mit Einführungssatz im Präsens (*Indirect speech with reporting verb in the present*)

●○○ 1. Wenn du direkt berichtest was jemand gesagt hat, ändern sich die Zeitformen nicht: für den Einführungssatz brauchst du das Präsens.
Du hast eine Weihnachtskarte von einer englischen Freundin bekommen. Erzähle was darin steht.

→ Lösung S. 122

Dear Anne,

I hope you and your family are well! It was lovely to see you last summer. I really enjoyed my visit. I have been working hard on my German since then, and it is getting much better!
I hope I will see you all again next summer.
Have a very happy Christmas!

Love from Lucy xxx

a) Lucy hopes ______

b) She says ______

c) She says ______

d) She writes ______

e) She hopes ______

f) She wishes us ______

●○○ 2. Bringe die Wörter in die richtige Reihenfolge und bilde Sätze in der indirekten Rede.

→ Lösung S. 122

a) she / us / says / later / call / Katie / will

______

b) enjoyed / we / Paul / party / the / hopes

______

4 Fragen in der indirekten Rede (*Indirect questions*)

●○○ 1. Wie wird die direkte Rede zur indirekten Rede? Kreuze an.

→ Lösung S. 122

a) "What time did you come home last night?"

Dad wanted to know
- ☐ what time we did come home last night.
- ☐ what time we came home last night.

b) "Where do you live?"

She asked me
- ☐ where I lived.
- ☐ where I do live.

c) "Have you finished the exercise?"

Our teacher asked us
- ☐ if we had finished the exercise.
- ☐ had we finished the exercise.

d) "Are you going to basketball training today?"

Ava wanted to know
- ☐ am I going to basketball training.
- ☐ whether I was going to basketball training.

●○○ 2. Schreibe die Fragen als indirekte Fragen um.

→ Lösung S. 122

a) "Will you help me translate this e-mail?"

Nina asked ______________________________

b) "Where did you lose your phone?"

Lenny asked ______________________________

c) "Who are you going to invite to your party?"

Mum wanted to know ______________________________

d) "Did you remember to send Greg a message?"

Susie asked ______________________________

●●○ 3. Die Schülerzeitung an deiner Schule hat dich interviewt, weil du ein Konzert für einen wohltätigen Zweck organisiert hast. Berichte in der indirekten Rede, was du gefragt wurdest.

→ Lösung S. 122

"Why did you organise the concert?"

"How many people came?"

"Was it difficult to organise?"

"Did you make a lot of money?"

"What kind of bands played at the concert?"

a) They asked me ______

b) ______

c) ______

d) ______

e) ______

●●○ 4. Ergänze die Sätze der indirekten Rede.

→ Lösung S. 122

a) "Can I have something to drink?"

She asked if / whether she could have ______ something to drink.

b) "Why did you leave Tom's party so early?"

He asked me ______ Tom's party so early.

c) "What time will you be home?"

She wanted to know ______ home.

d) "Have you ever visited London before?"

He asked ______ London before.

e) "Did you hear that noise?"

She asked me ______ that noise.

5 Veränderungen der Pronomen (*Pronoun changes*)

●○○ 1. Welches Pronomen ist richtig? → Lösung S. 122

a) "Can you send me John's phone number?" asked Julia.
Julia asked if she / I could send me / her John's phone number.

b) "You all have to come with me," said Mr Hammond.
Mr Hammond explained that he / we had to go with him / us.

c) "We'll see you on Saturday," said Dylan and Gracie.
Dylan and Gracie said he / they would see us / them on Saturday.

d) "Did you eat all of the pizza?" asked Jack.
Jack asked them / me if you / I had eaten all of the pizza.

e) "I'm going out with your sister," said Daniel.
Daniel told me / them that I / he was going out with his / my sister.

f) "Where are you going, Catherine?" I asked.
I asked you / her where she / I was going.

●●○ 2. Schreibe die Sätze in der indirekten Rede auf.
Achte darauf, dass die Pronomen stimmen. → Lösung S. 123

a) "Who can help me move this table?" asked Steven.

____

b) "My sister has just bought her first car," said Lisa.

____

c) "I took some great photos of you today!" I told Liam and Oscar.

____

d) "Grandma loves the flowers you sent her," I told my brother.

____

6 Zeitangaben in der indirekten Rede (*Time expressions in indirect speech*)

1. Ändere die Zeitangaben in den indirekten Sätzen. → Lösung S. 123

a) "My brother is starting a new job next week."
Hannah told us her brother was starting a new job
_______________________ .

b) "We didn't go on holiday last year."
He said that they hadn't gone on holiday _______________________ .

c) "We're going to have a lot of fun tonight!"
Becky promised that we were going to have a lot of fun
_______________________ .

d) "The children watch too much TV yesterday."
She said that the children had watched too much TV
_______________________ .

2. Oft müssen nicht nur die Zeitangaben angepasst werden. Schreibe die Sätze um und achte besonders auf die Wörter, die unterstrichen wurden. → Lösung S. 123

a) "I really like living <u>here</u>."
She said ____

b) "Oh! <u>These</u> cats are so sweet!"
He ____

c) "Are you <u>coming</u> to see Linda's band?"
She asked ____

d) "You will need to <u>bring</u> a pen and some paper."
He ____

●●○ 3. Es ist nicht immer notwendig, für die indirekte Rede die Zeitangabe zu ändern. Wenn der Tag, der Monat oder das Jahr noch nicht vorbei ist, musst du nichts ändern. Schaue genau auf die Informationen und schreibe indirekte Sätze.

→ Lösung S. 123

On 17th October, Leo said:

"I'll send you the link this evening."

"I have to have extra maths lessons this month."

"I don't have much time today."

On 17th October, Charlie said:

a) Leo said he ______________________________.

b) He told me ______________________________.

c) He said ______________________________.

On 5th November, Charlie said:

d) Leo said he ______________________________.

e) He told me ______________________________.

f) He said ______________________________.

●●○ 4. Achte auf die unterstrichenen Satzteile und wähle die richtige Alternative.

→ Lösung S. 123

a) They told me they had finished <u>this</u> / <u>that</u> project <u>two weeks ago</u> / <u>two weeks before</u>.

b) Jim said he would read <u>these</u> / <u>those</u> books <u>the next day</u> / <u>tomorrow</u>.

c) Stella asked us if we could <u>bring</u> / <u>take</u> some drinks to her party <u>next weekend</u> / <u>the following weekend</u>.

d) Martin said we had to <u>bring</u> / <u>take</u> enough money when we visited him because it was very expensive <u>here</u> / <u>there</u>.

7 Indirekte Aufforderungssätze (*Indirect commands*)

●○○ 1. Schreibe anhand der Wörter in Klammern indirekte Aufforderungen. → Lösung S. 123

a) "Stop making so much noise!" (he / tell / class)

____

b) "Be careful on the wet floor." (she / warn / everybody)

____

c) "Click on this link for more information." (he / tell / us)

____

d) "Write down all of the new words." (she / advise / them)

____

e) "Don't eat that!" (she / warn / me)

____

f) "Don't forget to call Sylvie." (she / remind / me)

____

●○○ 2. Bilde aus den Wörtern indirekte Aufforderungssätze. → Lösung S. 123

a) kids / Mum / their / reminded / to / teeth / the / clean

____

b) everyone / taste / told / Simon / his / to / cake

____

c) us / buy / soon / they / tickets / to / advised / the

____

d) warned / not / on / us / beach / go / to / they / the

____

1 Direkte und indirekte Rede (*Direct and indirect speech*)

Übungen ab S. 109

1. b) "What time does the film start?" asked Gracie. c) "I have never been to Italy," said Paul. d) "Have you seen my keys?" asked Janie. e) "There will be a German test tomorrow," said Mrs Braun.

2. a) "I'm getting a dog next week," said Claire. b) "I've got a new girlfriend," said Harry. c) "Can I borrow 5 euros?" asked Jonas.

3. a) Caroline **said** that she would be home late that evening. b) Mr Connors **told** us this is really good website for practising English grammar. c) Lara **promised** that she wouldn't tell my parents about the broken vase. d) Mrs Summers **explained** that the cafeteria was downstairs, opposite the secretary's office. e) He thanked us for coming and **added** that it had been nice to meet us. f) We asked if she wanted to come with us, but she **answered** that she didn't have time. g) He **wanted to know** what time the film started.

4. a) He told me his brother works in a bank. b) He told me his old dog died last year. c) He told me he's going to university in September. d) He told me he doesn't live in Elder Street now.

2 Veränderung der Zeitform (*Tense change*)

Übungen ab S. 111

1. a) The children said that they were hungry. b) Christina said that she didn't think it was a good idea. c) Joanna promised that she would call me later. d) Caroline told me that Ted wouldn't like that photo. e) Richard said that he didn't want to talk to me. f) Dawn said that they were having a really great holiday.

2. a) He said he **had lived** in China for three years. b) She explained that Angela **hadn't given** her my message. c) She said she **hadn't cleaned** her room yet. d) He said someone **had eaten** all the cookies.

3. a) Sam said he'd got three cats. b) Sam said he could play the violin. c) Sam said he had been to Florida the year before. d) Sam said he had never been to the USA before. e) Sam said he had met lots of famous people. f) Sam said he was having a big party on his next birthday.

4. a) She said she **had sent** Andy a lot of texts. b) ☑ c) She said it **would be** very cold the next day. d) ☑ e) She said they **had been waiting** for a long time.

5. a) "I'm very popular with my fans," said Robbie. b) "I'm not allowed to drink coffee," said Susie. c) "I'm coming to your party," said Angie. d) "I haven't studied for the test," said Tom.

3 Die indirekte Rede mit Einführungssatz im Präsens (*Indirect speech with reporting verb in the present*)

Übungen ab S. 114

1. a) Lucy hopes we are well. b) She says it was lovely to see us last summer. c) She says she really enjoyed her visit. d) She writes that she has been working hard on her German and that it is getting much better. e) She hopes she will see us again next summer. f) She wishes us a very happy Christmas.

2. a) Katie says she will call us later. b) Paul hopes we enjoyed the party.

4 Fragen in der indirekten Rede (*Indirect questions*)

Übungen ab S. 115

1. a) Dad wanted to know what time we came home last night. b) She asked me where I lived. c) Our teacher asked us if we had finished the exercise. d) Ava wanted to know whether I was going to basketball training.

2. a) Nina asked if I would help her translate that e-mail. b) Lenny asked where I had lost my phone. c) Mum wanted to know who I was going to invite to my party. d) Susie asked if I had remembered to send Greg a message.

3. a) They asked me why I had organised the concert. b) They asked if/whether it had been difficult to organise. c) They asked me how many people had come. d) They asked me what kind of bands had played at the concert. e) They asked me if/whether we made a lot of money.

4. b) He asked me **why I had left** Tom's party so early. c) She wanted to know **what time I would be** home. d) He asked **if/whether I had ever visited** London before. e) She asked me **if/whether I had heard** that noise.

5 Veränderungen der Pronomen (*Pronoun changes*)

Übungen ab S. 117

1. a) Julia asked if **I** could send **her** John's phone number. b) Mr Hammond explained that **we** had to go with **him**. c) Dylan and Gracie said **they** would see **us** on Saturday. d) Jack asked **me** if **I** had eaten all of the pizza. e) Daniel told **me** that **he** was going out with **my** sister. f) I asked **her** where **she** was going.

2. a) Steven asked who could help him move that table. b) Lisa said her sister had just bought her first car. c) I told Liam and Oscar that I had taken some great photos of them that day. d) I told my brother that Grandma loved the flowers he had sent her.

6 Zeitangaben in der indirekten Rede (*Time expressions in indirect speech*)

→ Übungen ab S. 118

1. a) Hannah told us her brother was starting a new job **the following week**. b) He said that they hadn't gone on holiday **the year before**. c) Becky promised that we were going to have a lot of fun **that night**. d) She said that the children had watched too much TV **the day before**.

2. a) She said she really liked living **there**. b) He said **those** cats were so sweet. c) She asked if I was **going** to see Linda's band. d) He said I/we would need to **take** a pen and some paper.

3. a) Leo said he would send me the link **this evening**. b) He told me that he had to have extra maths lessons **this month**. c) He said that he didn't have much time **today**. d) Leo said he would send me the link **that evening**. e) He told me that he had to have extra maths lessons **last month**. f) He said that he didn't have much time **that day**.

4. a) They told me they had finished **that** project **two weeks before**. b) Jim said he would read **those** books **the next day**. c) Stella asked us if we could **take** some drinks to her party **the following weekend**. d) Martin said we had to **take** enough money when we visited him because it was very expensive **there**.

7 Indirekte Aufforderungssätze (*Indirect commands*)

→ Übungen ab S. 120

1. a) He told the class to stop making so much noise. b) She warned everybody to be careful on the wet floor. c) He told us to click on that link for more information. d) She advised them to write down all of the new words. e) She warned me not to eat that. f) She reminded me to call Sylvie.

2. a) Mum reminded the kids to clean their teeth. b) Simon told everyone to taste his cake. c) They advised us to buy the tickets soon. d) They warned us not to go on the beach.

Relativsätze (*Relative clauses*)

1 Relativpronomen (*Relative pronouns*)

●○○ 1. Füge die Relativpronomen (*who / that / which / whose / whom*) in den folgenden Sätzen ein. → Lösung S. 132

a) That's the girl ____________ I met at the theatre club last week.

b) There's an article about the school ____________ I go to in the newspaper.

c) The Thompsons are the people ____________ cat we are looking after.

d) Are you the person to ____________ I spoke on the phone yesterday?

e) The church ____________ is on the corner of our street is very old.

f) That's the girl ____________ scored the winning goal.

g) This is a song ____________ is very popular at the moment – they play it all the time on the radio.

h) We are looking for someone ____________ can design a new website for our club.

●●○ 2. Kann man das auch so sagen? Lies diese Relativsätze und verbessere die Fehler, die du findest. Ein Satz ist korrekt. → Lösung S. 132

a) Pizza is something what a lot of people like eating.

b) That's the shop who sells those really expensive headphones.

c) A vegetarian is a person whom doesn't eat meat.

d) Mr Harland is the teacher who never gives us homework on Fridays.

e) A doctor is someone helps sick people.

f) I've got a friend which comes from Scotland.

2 Notwendige Relativsätze (*Defining relative clauses*)

●○○ 1. Verbinde die Satzteile, die zusammenpassen. → Lösung S. 132

a) Do you know anyone	that downloaded the virus.
b) This is the question	who posted those photos.
c) Claire is the girl	which won the championship.
d) Japan is a country	who could mend my laptop for me?
e) Yes, it was my brother	whose school was on fire.
f) I played in the team	that makes bread and cakes.
g) It was Maria	whose dad is driving us to the match.
h) We were waiting for the bus	that is the most difficult to answer.
i) Those are the kids	whose culture is very old.
j) A baker is someone	that goes to the city centre.

●○○ 2. Ordne die Wörter so, dass du einen Relativsatz bilden kannst. → Lösung S. 132

a) always / the / me / that's / barks / that / at / dog

____

b) Australian / is / know / whose / I / someone / mother

____

c) knows / this / everybody / is / which / song / a

____

d) the / married / who / President / the / she's / woman

____

e) late / ones / you / always / are / who / the / are

____

●●○ 3. Verbinde die beiden Sätzen durch ein Relativpronomen miteinander. → Lösung S. 132

a) Dylan's got a sister. Her name is Gracie.

Dylan's got a sister whose name is Gracie.

b) We live in a house. The house is 100 years old.

____

c) Paula was wearing a jacket. The jacket was very old.

____

d) I knew a girl. The girl was on a casting show.

____

e) We visited a museum. It was very interesting.

____

f) I had a teacher. His son was in my class.

____

●●○ 4. Übertrage die Relativsätze ins Deutsch. → Lösung S. 132

a) Jenny found some money that was lying on the street.

____

b) Where are the keys which were on the table?

____

c) That's the boy who broke his leg last week.

____

d) I know someone whose aunt is a film star.

____

3 Präpositionen im notwendigen Relativsatz (*Prepositions in defining relative clauses*)

●○○ 1. Kreuze das richtige Satzende an. → Lösung S. 133

a) Who's that girl ______ ?

☐ to who is talking Sean? ☐ who Sean is talking to

b) This is the hotel ______ when we were in Italy.

☐ that we stayed in ☐ in what we stayed

c) Paul is one of the boys ______ .

☐ whom with I went to school ☐ with whom I went to school.

d) The house ______ is near here.

☐ in which I grew up ☐ which I grew up

e) I've got a laptop ______ .

☐ that I play games on ☐ on that I play games

●●○ 2. Schreibe die Sätze wie in dem Beispiel um. → Lösung S. 133

a) The dog played with this ball.

This is the ball that/which the dog played with.

b) I spoke to a woman who had climbed Mount Everest.

The woman ______

c) We were waiting in a very dark room.

The room ______

d) She cut the bread with this knife.

This is ______

4 Relativsätze ohne Relativpronomen (*Contact clauses*)

●○○ 1. Verbinde die beiden Sätze zu einem langen Satz.
Hier benötigst du kein Relativpronomen. → Lösung S. 133

a) I met a girl on holiday. She still writes to me.

The girl I met on holiday still writes to me.

b) Tom sent me a message. I didn't get the message.

I didn't get ______

c) He ate some fish. It made him sick.

The fish ______

d) We saw a film. It was very boring.

The film ______

e) I lost a key last week. I've just found it.

I've ______

f) We gave Jackie a present. She really liked it.

Jackie ______

●○○ 2. Bringe die Wörter in die richtige Reihenfolge. → Lösung S. 133

a) us / did / exercises / we / teacher / the / gave / our

______

b) sent / liked / the / granny / we / her / flowers

______

c) boy / week / the / I / that's / met / last

______

d) had / dog / the / made / I / cookies / ate / the

______

●●○ 3. Verwende die Aussagen, die in den bunten Kästen stehen, um Relativsätze zu bilden. → Lösung S. 133

Marc sent me a link

~~I bought some concert tickets~~

Joshua told me a story

We had an English test last week

I was invited to a party

I sent Maria a card

a) The concert tickets I bought were very expensive.

b) The English test ______ was quite easy.

c) I couldn't go to the party ______.

d) I opened the link ______.

e) Maria loved the card ______.

f) The story ______ wasn't true.

●●○ 4. Bilde aus den Stichwörtern Relativsätze ohne Relativpronomen. → Lösung S. 133

a) in my class / she is talking to / is / the girl

______

b) were / we stayed with / the people / very friendly

______

c) you are making / smells / the cake / delicious

______

5 Gemischte Aufgaben (*Mixed forms*)

●○○ 1. Brauchst du in diesen Sätzen ein Relativpronomen? Falls nicht, streiche es durch.

→ Lösung S. 133

a) The tree that was in our garden fell down in the storm.

b) I didn't read the book that you gave me.

c) The woman who we met on holiday lives very near us.

d) A woman who lives in our street was on TV last week.

e) Do you know anyone who can help me fix my bike?

f) Mrs Martin gave us a list of the words which we have to learn.

g) She saw a film that changed her life.

h) He was the best friend that I ever had.

i) Are these the shirts that are for the football team?

j) Pupils don't like teachers who give them too much homework.

●○○ 2. Findest du die Fehler, die sich hier eingeschlichen haben? Auch ein Komma kann falsch sein. Schreibe die Sätze korrekt auf.

→ Lösung S. 133

a) That's a song is difficult to sing.

____

b) They're looking for someone, who speaks Japanese.

____

c) He's the teacher which tells a lot of jokes during the lesson.

____

d) The e-mail address, that you gave me, is wrong.

____

●●○ 3. Verbinde immer zwei Satzteile, um Relativsätze zu bilden.
Ergänze ein Relativpronomen, wenn nötig. → Lösung S. 134

a) Do you know the girl	______	I lent her.
b) The police found the thief	______	he saw last week.
c) Ella lost the book	______	Sally's talking to?
d) I'm looking for someone	______	we had to learn?
e) A bird is an animal	______	I took yesterday.
f) Tom didn't enjoy the film	______	stole my bike.
g) Can you remember the new words	______	don't eat any animal products.
h) What's the name of the song	______	can feed my cat next weekend.
i) Vegans are people	______	can fly.
j) These are the photos	______	Ed Sheeran sings?

●●○ 4. Bilde Relativsätze aus den zwei Sätzen.
Verwende Relativpronomen nur, wo es nötig ist. → Lösung S. 134

a) Kim writes blog posts every week. They are really funny.

The blog posts ______________________________

b) A boy was hurt in the accident. He's OK now.

____

c) A tree fell down in the storm. It was very old.

____

d) I spoke to a woman. She was very unfriendly.

____

1 Relativpronomen (*Relative pronouns*)

Übungen ab S. 124

1. a) That's the girl **who / that** I met at the theatre club last week. b) There's an article about the school **that / which** I go to in the newspaper. c) The Thompsons are the people **whose** cat we are looking after. d) Are you the person to **whom** I spoke on the phone yesterday? e) The church **that / which** is on the corner of our street is very old. f) That's the girl **who / that** scored the winning goal. g) This is a song **that / which** is very popular at the moment – they play it all the time on the radio. h) We are looking for someone **who / that** can design a new website for our club.

2. a) Pizza is something **that / which** a lot of people like eating. b) That's the shop **that / which** sells those really expensive headphones. c) A vegetarian is a person **who / that** doesn't eat meat. d) ☑ e) A doctor is someone **who / that** helps sick people. f) I've got a friend **who** comes from Scotland.

2 Notwendige Relativsätze (*Defining relative clauses*)

Übungen ab S. 125

1. a) Do you know anyone who could mend my laptop for me? b) This is the question that is the most difficult to answer. c) Claire is the girl whose dad is driving us to the match. d) Japan is a country whose culture is very old. e) Yes, it was my brother that downloaded the virus. f) I played in the team which won the championship. g) It was Maria who posted those photos. h) We were waiting for the bus that goes to the city centre. i) Those are the kids whose school was on fire. j) A baker is someone that makes bread and cakes.

2. a) That's the dog that always barks at me. b) I know someone whose mother is Australian. c) This is a song which everybody knows. d) She's the woman who married the President. e) You are the ones who are always late.

3. b) We live in a house that / which is 100 years old. c) Paula was wearing a jacket that / which was very old. d) I knew a girl who / that was on a casting show. e) We visited a museum that / which was very interesting. f) I had a teacher whose son was in my class.

4. a) Jenny hat Geld gefunden, das auf der Straße lag. b) Wo sind die Schlüssel, die auf dem Tisch waren? c) Das ist der Junge, der sich letzte Woche das Bein gebrochen hat. d) Ich kenne jemand, dessen Tante Filmstar ist.

3 Präpositionen im notwendigen Relativsatz (*Prepositions in defining relative clauses*)

→ Übungen ab S. 127

1. a) Who's that girl **who Sean is talking to**? b) This is the hotel **that we stayed in** when we were in Italy. c) Paul is one of the boys **with whom I went to school**. d) The house **in which I grew up** is near here. e) I've got a laptop **that I play games on**.

2. b) The woman I spoke to had climbed Mount Everest. c) The room we were waiting in was very dark. d) This is the knife she cut the bread with.

4 Relativsätze ohne Relativpronomen (*Contact clauses*)

→ Übungen ab S. 128

1. b) I didn't get the message Tom sent me. c) The fish he ate made him sick. d) The film we saw was very boring. e) I've just found the key I lost last week. f) Jackie really liked the present we gave her.

2. a) We did the exercises our teacher gave us. b) Granny liked the flowers we sent her. c) That's the boy I met last week. d) The dog ate the cookies I had made.

3. b) The English test **we had last week** was quite easy. c) I couldn't go to the party **I was invited to**. d) I opened the link **Marc sent me**. e) Maria loved the card **I sent her**. f) The story **Joshua told me** wasn't true.

4. a) The girl she is talking to is in my class. b) The people we stayed with were very friendly. c) The cake you are making smells delicious.

5 Gemischte Aufgaben (*Mixed forms*)

→ Übungen ab S. 130

1. a) The tree **that** was in our garden fell down in the storm. b) I didn't read the book ~~that~~ you gave me. c) The woman ~~who~~ we met on holiday lives very near us. d) A woman **who** lives in our street was on TV last week. e) Do you know anyone **who** can help me fix my bike? f) Mrs Martin gave us a list of the words ~~which~~ we have to learn. g) She saw a film **that** changed her life. h) He was the best friend ~~that~~ I ever had. i) Are these the shirts **that** are for the football team? j) Pupils don't like teachers **who** give them too much homework.

2. a) That's a song **that/which** is difficult to sing. b) They're looking for **someone who** speaks Japanese. c) He's the teacher **who/that** tells a lot of jokes during the lesson. d) The e-mail **address that** you gave **me is** wrong.

3. a) Do you know the girl **who / that** Sally's talking to? b) The police found the thief **who / that** stole my bike. c) Ella lost the book I lent her. d) I'm looking for someone **who / that** can feed my cat next weekend. e) A bird is an animal **that / which** can fly. f) Tom didn't enjoy the film he saw last week. g) Can you remember the new words we had to learn? h) What's the name of the song Ed Sheeran sings? i) Vegans are people **who / that** don't eat any animal products. J) These are the photos I took yesterday.

4. a) The blog posts Kim writes every week are really funny. b) The boy who / that was hurt in the accident is OK now. c) The tree that / which fell down in the storm was very old. d) The woman I spoke to was very unfriendly.

Das Passiv (*The passive*)

1 Aktiv und Passiv (*Active and passive*)

●○○ 1. Welche der folgenden Sätze sind aktiv und welche sind passiv? Schreibe auf die Linie.

→ Lösung S. 144

a) I forgot to feed my goldfish. ______________

b) The classrooms are cleaned every evening. ______________

c) The play was written by Berthold Brecht. ______________

d) Shakespeare wrote some of the world's most famous plays. ______________

e) We'll help you get ready for the party. ______________

f) A prize will be given for the best photo. ______________

g) A lot of money has been spent on the new building. ______________

●○○ 2. Ergänze die Sätze. Benutze Aktiv oder Passiv, je nachdem, was zu den Bildern passt.

→ Lösung S. 144

a) Ice-cream ______________________________ here. (*to sell*)

b) She ______________________________ ice-cream. (*to sell*)

c) Marie ______________________________ French. (*to speak*)

d) English ______________________________ here. (*to speak*)

●●○ 3. Schreibe diese Sätze um. Der Aktivsatz soll jeweils passiv werden und der Passivsatz aktiv. Achte dabei auf die Zeitform!

→ Lösung S. 144

a) I lost my phone.

My phone ______________________________

b) All the sandwiches had been eaten.

Somebody ______________________________

c) They clean the windows every month.

____

d) Somebody has stolen Cathy's bike.

____

e) People drink a lot of coffee in Italy.

____

f) The tickets will be sold on Wednesday afternoon.

____

g) People often wear traditional clothes at weddings.

____

●●○ 4. Entscheide, ob die Sätze aktiv oder passiv sind und füge die richtige Verbform ein.

→ Lösung S. 144

a) Simon ______________ us a funny story about his dog. (*tell*)

b) We ______________ to wait here. (*tell*)

c) Football ______________ nearly everywhere in the world. (*play*)

d) Helen ______________ football every Saturday morning. (*play*)

e) A dictionary ______________ for checking words. (*use*)

f) We are not allowed to ______________ a dictionary in the test. (*use*)

2 Das Passiv: Form und Gebrauch (*The passive: forms and use*)

●○○ 1. Füge das richtige Verb im Passiv ein. Verwende entweder das *present simple* oder das *past simple*.

→ Lösung S. 144

build • eat • find • invent • invite • make • send • use

a) These Roman coins ____________________ in somebody's garden.

b) Pizza ____________________ in nearly every country in the world.

c) Millions of text messages ____________________ every day.

d) Mobile phones ____________________ about 40 years ago.

e) These cookies ____________________ with brown sugar and chocolate chips.

f) The castle ____________________ in 1658.

g) This machine ____________________ to store information.

h) Tony ____________________ to the party but he didn't go.

●○○ 2. Schreibe Fragen in der Passiv-Form, die zu diesen Antworten passen.

→ Lösung S. 144

a) Where ____?

These photos were taken on our holiday in Croatia.

b) ____?

No, the e-mail hasn't been sent yet.

c) ____?

Yes, the missing cat has been found.

d) ____?

This ring is made of silver.

e) ____?

No, nobody was hurt in the accident.

●○○ 3. Verbinde die Satzteile, die zusammenpassen. → Lösung S. 144

a) In Britain, tea is often	translated into many languages.
b) No, sorry, the work won't be	trained to help blind people.
c) French and English are	told hundreds of years ago.
d) This book has been	drunk with milk.
e) On my last birthday, I was	he was stopped by the police.
f) The dogs had been	finished until next week.
g) The message was	given their medals.
h) These stories were first	spoken in Canada.
i) Tom was driving home when	sent to me yesterday evening.
j) The winners had already been	given some great presents.

●●○ 4. Das Passiv wird oft für Zeitungsberichte benutzt.
Ergänze diesen Artikel aus einer Schülerzeitung
mit Passiv-Verben in der richtigen Zeitform. → Lösung S. 144

A mysterious visitor

Strange things have been happening in 7D's classroom this week.
On Monday night, a water bottle a) ______________________ (break) and there was water all over the floor.
On Wednesday morning, the class saw that books and papers b) ______________________ (push) off a desk during the night.
As well as that, somebody's scarf c) ______________________ (tear) and an old sandwich d) ______________________ (take) from a desk and e) ______________________ (eat) – well, part of it. The rest f) ______________________ (leave) under a chair.
At first, the class could not imagine who their night-time visitor could be. However, the mystery g) ______________________ just ______________________ (solve).
The windows h) ______________________ (open) every evening for half an hour or so after the room i) ______________________ (clean), and the caretaker's cat has been coming in to take a look around!

3 Das Passiv bei Verben mit zwei Objekten (*Passive sentences with two objects*)

●●○ 1. Von einem Aktivsatz, der zwei Objekte hat, kannst du zwei Passivsätze bilden – beginne jeweils mit einem der beiden Objekte und schreibe beide mögliche Passivsätze auf. → Lösung S. 145

a) Tom's parents promised him a new computer.

Tom was promised a new computer (by his parents).

A new computer was promised to Tom.

b) They showed us a film.

____

____

c) People often send me texts.

____

____

d) Grandad showed us all of his holiday photos.

____

____

●●○ 2. Schreibe diese Passivsätze in die Form des persönlichen Passivs um. → Lösung S. 145

a) A prize was given to them.

____

b) A great job was offered to my brother.

____

c) Some beautiful flowers were sent to Alice.

____

4 Passivsätze mit *by* (*Passive sentences with 'by'*)

●○○ 1. Ändere die Aktiv- in Passivsätze um, das Subjekt soll dabei mit *by* ergänzt werden (*by* agent). → Lösung S. 145

a) The Queen will open the new museum next week.

____

b) Millions of people speak English.

____

c) My dad mended my bike.

____

d) A famous architect designed this building.

____

e) Two people saw the accident.

____

f) Elton John wrote the music for this film.

____

●○○ 2. Beantworte die Fragen im Passiv. → Lösung S. 145

a) Who wrote this story? (Mike)

This story ______________________________

b) Who sings "Someone like you"? (Adele)

____

c) Who made these cookies? (Jason)

____

d) Who will take the photos tomorrow? (Katie)

____

●●○ 3. Schreibe Passivsätze im *simple past* mit *by*. Verwende dabei Elemente aus allen drei Spalten der Tabelle.

→ Lösung S. 145

a) ~~"Romeo and Juliet"~~	build	Leonardo da Vinci
b) The World Cup	celebrate	Tim Berners-Lee
c) The Pyramids	~~write~~	Germany in 2014.
d) The "Mona Lisa"	sing	Christians around the world
e) The internet	discover	~~Shakespeare~~
f) Christmas	win	the Vikings
g) "Yellow Submarine"	invent	Egyptians
h) America	paint	the Beatles

a) "Romeo and Juliet" was written by Shakespeare.

b) ______

c) ______

d) ______

e) ______

f) ______

g) ______

h) ______

●●○ 4. Wie heißt das auf Deutsch? Übersetze diese Passivsätze.

→ Lösung S. 145

a) The picture was painted by my sister.

______

b) The rooms are cleaned by Mrs Jones.

______

c) My phone was stolen by a thief.

______

d) The film was made by Steven Spielberg.

______

5 Gemischte Aufgaben (*Mixed forms*)

●○○ 1. Schreibe die Sätze in Passivsätze um und überlege dabei, ob es notwendig ist, den Verursacher der Handlung zu nennen. Falls ja, benutze *by*. → Lösung S. 145

a) The Romans built this old road.

____

b) They don't sell food in post offices.

____

c) Nobody invited Andrew to the party.

____

d) Do you know where they grow coffee?

____

e) The British team won the competition.

____

f) My friend Ben will direct the film "The Day of the Lion."

____

●○○ 2. Ergänze die Sätze mit dem Verb im Aktiv oder Passiv. → Lösung S. 146

a) James ____________ a lot of money on clothes. (spend)

b) A lot of money ____________ on the new shopping centre. (spend)

c) Who ____________ these photos? (take)

d) Where ______ these photos ________ ? (take)

e) A lot of films ____________ in Hollywood. (make)

f) Where ______ they ________ the new James Bond film? (make)

g) This knife ____________ to cut bread. (use)

h) She ____________ a sharp knife to open the box. (use)

●○○ 3. Welcher Satz macht in diesen Beispielen mehr Sinn: die aktive oder die passive Version? Kreuze an. → Lösung S. 146

a) ☐ John has visited a lot of different countries.
☐ A lot of different countries have been visited by John.

b) ☐ This house is very old. Somebody built it in 1700.
☐ This house is very old. It was built in 1700.

c) ☐ Charlie lost his phone last week.
☐ The phone was lost by Charlie last week.

d) ☐ When did somebody invent the telephone?
☐ When was the telephone invented?

e) ☐ Annie is very popular. Everybody likes her.
☐ Annie is very popular. She is liked by everybody.

f) ☐ Where do they grow rice?
☐ Where is rice grown?

●●○ 4. Schreibe selber Passivsätze mit den Stichwörtern. → Lösung S. 146

a) this ring / give / me / my grandmother

This ring was ______________________________

b) the story / we / tell / wasn't true

____

c) the books / send / you / tomorrow

____

d) my jacket / take! / I can't find it!

____

e) our old house / buy / a family / from Wales

____

1 Aktiv und Passiv (*Active and passive*)

Übungen ab S. 135

1. a) active b) passive c) passive d) active e) active f) passive g) passive

2. a) Ice-cream **is sold** here. b) She **is selling** ice-cream. c) Marie **speaks** French. d) English **is spoken** at this hotel.

3. a) My phone was lost. b) Somebody had eaten all the sandwiches. c) The windows are cleaned every month. d) Cathy's bike has been stolen. e) A lot of coffee is drunk in Italy. f) They will sell the tickets on Wednesday afternoon. g) Traditional clothes are often worn at weddings.

4. a) Simon **told** us a funny story about his dog. b) We **were told** to wait here. c) Football **is played** nearly everywhere in the world. d) Helen **plays** football every Saturday morning. e) A dictionary **is used** for checking words. f) We are not allowed to **use** a dictionary in the test.

2 Das Passiv: Form und Gebrauch (*The passive: forms and use*)

Übungen ab S. 137

1. a) These Roman coins **were found** in somebody's garden. b) Pizza **is eaten** in nearly every country in the world. c) Millions of text messages **are sent** every day. d) Mobile phones **were invented** about 40 years ago. e) These cookies **are made** with brown sugar and chocolate chips. f) The castle **was built** in 1658. g) This machine **is used** to store information. h) Tony **was invited** to the party but he didn't go.

2. a) Where were these photos taken? b) Has the e-mail been sent yet? c) Has the missing cat been found? d) What is this ring made of? e) Was anybody hurt in the accident?

3. a) In Britain, tea is often drunk with milk. b) No, sorry, the work won't be finished until next week. c) French and English are spoken in Canada. d) This book has been translated into many languages. e) On my last birthday, I was given some great presents. f) The dogs had been trained to help blind people. g) The message was sent to me yesterday evening. h) These stories were first told hundreds of years ago. i) Tom was driving home when he was stopped by the police. j) The winners had already been given their medals.

4. Strange things have been happening in 7D's classroom this week. On Monday night, a water bottle a) **was broken** and there was water all over the floor. On Wednesday morning, the class saw that books and papers b) **had been pushed** off a desk during the night. As well as that, somebody's scarf c) **had been torn** and an old sandwich d) **had been taken** from a desk and e) **eaten** – well, part of it. The rest f) **had been left** under a chair. At first, the class could not imagine who their night-time visitor could be. However, the mystery g) **has** just **been solved**. The windows h) **are opened** every evening for half an hour or so after the room i) **has been cleaned**, and the caretaker's cat has been coming in to take a look around!

3 Das Passiv bei Verben mit zwei Objekten (Passive sentences with two objects)

→ Übungen ab S. 139

1. b) We were shown a film. A film was shown to us. c) I am often sent texts. Texts are often sent to me. d) We were shown all of Grandad's holiday photos. All of Grandad's holiday photos were shown to us.

2. a) They were given a prize. b) My brother was offered a great job. c) Alice was sent some beautiful flowers.

4 Passivsätze mit *by* (Passive sentences with 'by')

→ Übungen ab S. 140

1. a) The new museum will be opened by the Queen next week. b) English is spoken by millions of people. c) My bike was mended by my dad. d) This building was designed by a famous architect. e) The accident was seen by two people. f) The music for this film was written by Elton John.

2. a) This story was written by Mike. b) "Someone like you" is sung by Adele. c) These cookies were made by Jason. d) The photos will be taken by Katie tomorrow.

3. b) The World Cup was won by Germany in 2014. c) The Pyramids were built by the Egyptians. d) The "Mona Lisa" was painted by Leonardo da Vinci. e) The internet was invented by Tim Berners-Lee. f) Christmas is celebrated by Christians around the world. g) "Yellow Submarine" was sung by the Beatles. h) America was discovered by the Vikings.

4. a) Das Bild wurde von meiner Schwester gemalt. b) Die Zimmer werden von Mrs Jones geputzt. c) Mein Telefon wurde von einem Dieb gestohlen. d) Der Film wurde von Steven Spielberg gemacht.

5 Gemischte Aufgaben (*Mixed forms*)

→ Übungen ab S.142

1. a) This old road was built by the Romans. b) Food isn't sold in post offices. c) Andrew wasn't invited to the party. d) Do you know where coffee is grown? e) The competition was won by the British team. f) The film "The Day of the Lion" will be directed by my friend Ben.

2. a) James **spends** a lot of money on clothes. b) A lot of money **was spent** on the new shopping centre. c) Who **took** these photos? d) Where **were** these photos **taken**? e) A lot of films **are made** in Hollywood. f) Where **are** they **making** / Where **did** they **make** the new James Bond film? g) This knife **is used** to cut bread. h) She **used** a sharp knife to open the box.

3. a) John has visited a lot of different countries. b) This house is very old. It was built in 1700. c) Charlie lost his phone last week. d) When was the telephone invented? e) Annie is very popular. Everybody likes her. f) Where is rice grown?

4. a) This ring was given to me by my grandmother. b) The story we were told wasn't true. c) The books will be sent to you tomorrow. d) My jacket has been taken! I can't find it! e) Our old house was bought by a family from Wales.

TEXTVERSTÄNDNIS

In der Stadt (*Towns and cities*)

1 Wortschatz: Verkehr und Verkehrsmittel (*Vocabulary: Traffic and transport*)

●○○ 1. Löse das Kreuzworträtsel und finde das Lösungswort. → Lösung S. 157

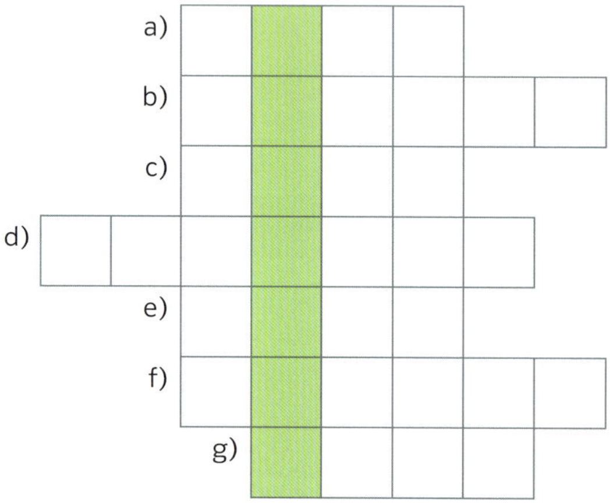

Lösungswort: ☐☐☐☐☐☐☐

a) If the last bus has left, we'll have to take a ________________ .

b) You can buy a ________________ from the bus driver.

c) A ________________ is a boat that travels short distances, for example across a river.

d) If you are in town all week, a ________________ is cheaper than buying a ticket every day.

e) I would love to sail around the world in my own ________________ .

f) Tower ________________ crosses the River Thames.

g) A ________________ is a bit like a train that drives along the street.

●○○ 2. Ergänze die Sätze mit einem der vorgegebenen Wörter.

→ Lösung S. 157

bike • bus • foot • helicopter • plane • platform • station • traffic • tunnel • underground

a) The train to Birmingham leaves from ________________ 4.

b) Excuse me, does this ________________ go to the city centre?

c) Catherine doesn't like travelling by ________________ because she's nervous about flying.

d) They're building a new ________________ under the river.

e) It was a very bad accident. Two people were flown to hospital by ________________ .

f) We were late because there was a lot of ________________ .

g) Most big cities have ________________ trains. They are a fast way to travel around the city.

h) We need to hurry to the ________________ . Our train leaves in 10 minutes!

i) This map is helpful if you want to tour the city on ________________ .

j) Charlie rides his ________________ every day, even in bad weather.

●○○ 3. Welche Wörter passen zusammen? Verbinde die Begriffe.

→ Lösung S. 157

a) bus	map	transport	b) underground
f) train	platform	lights	c) ticket
g) Tube	train	station	h) northbound
e) traffic	machine	pass	d) public

●○○ 4. Kreuze jeweils das Verb an, das am besten passt. → Lösung S. 157

a) What time does this train ______ Paddington?

☐ arrive at ☐ go by ☐ wait for

b) Jack arrived late because he ______ the wrong bus.

☐ went with ☐ got on ☐ arrived at

c) Take the number 37 bus to the town hall and then ______ to the 63.

☐ drive over ☐ take ☐ change

d) How long have we been ______ the tram? It's 20 minutes late!

☐ getting on ☐ waiting for ☐ going by

e) It was difficult to ______ the train with my big suitcase.

☐ get off ☐ drive with ☐ wait for

f) We had a great view of the city as we ______ the bridge.

☐ changed to ☐ arrived at ☐ drove over

●●○ 5. Finde und verbessere die Fehler, die sich in diese Sätze hinein geschlichen haben. → Lösung S. 157

a) Alex drives with the train to school every day.

____

b) Linda gets out the bus two stops before me.

____

c) Shall we go to town by bike or to foot?

____

d) Please buy a card before you get on the train.

____

2 Eine Anzeige am Bahnhof verstehen (*Understanding station announcements*)

●○○ 1. Ergänze die Sätze mit den fehlenden Informationen. → Lösung S. 157

1

a) The train now arriving at platform ________ is the 10.15 to London Paddington.

b) The ________ to Bristol Temple Meads is now arriving at platform 5. This train stops at Swindon, ________ Spa and Bristol Temple Meads.

c) Platform change: the 9.03 to Birmingham New Street will now leave from platform ________ , not platform ________ .

d) The 17.46 to York will be ________ minutes late. We apologise for the late arrival of this service.

●●○ 2. Du bist mit deinen Eltern in England im Urlaub. Ihr reist mit dem Zug und steht gerade am Bahnhof. Ihr hört eine Lautsprecheransage, aber deine Eltern verstehen nicht alles. Hilf Ihnen und beantworte ihre Fragen. → Lösung S. 158

2

Mama: Ich habe Edinburgh verstanden. Da fahren wir ja hin! Heißt das, der Zug ist pünktlich?

Du: a) Nein, ____ .

Mama: Aber warum?

Du: b) ____ .

Mama: Und wie lang dauert das jetzt alles?

Du: c) ____ .

Mama: Was sollen wir jetzt machen?

Du: d) ____ .

Scanne den QR-Code und höre den Text an.

3 Sehenswürdigkeiten (*Sightseeing and attractions*)

●○○ 1. Höre dir diese Beschreibung über Edinburgh Castle an und ergänze die fehlenden Wörter.

3

→ Lösung S. 158

Edinburgh Castle stands on Castle a) ________________ .

There has been a royal castle there since around the b) ________________ century. Kings and queens lived there until c) ________________ . After that, the Castle stopped being a home for royalty, but it was still important for the military. It was difficult to d) ________________ the Castle because it stands on a e) ________________ . Its walls are made of thick f) ________________ , which helped the Castle to survive hundreds of years of Scottish weather!

Today, Edinburgh Castle is the most popular tourist g) ________________ in Scotland. Around h) ________________ people visit it every year. Visitors can take a guided tour or listen to information on i) ________________ as they walk around. In some rooms, there are actors who bring the Castle's history to life.

Scanne den QR-Code und höre den Text an.

One of the biggest attractions at Edinburgh Castle is the j) ________________ Gun. Every day, at 1 in the afternoon, a large gun is fired over the wall of the castle. This tradition started in 1861 and was done so that k) ________________ on the sea near Edinburgh would know the correct time. The Castle is also famous for the Edinburgh Military Tattoo, which is a performance by groups of military bands, mostly with pipes[1] and drums. It takes place in l) ________________ every year.

[1] Dudelsack

●○○ 2. Hör dir die Informationen über Edinburgh Castle noch einmal an und kreuze an, ob die Aussagen richtig oder falsch sind, oder ob sie nicht erwähnt wurden.

3

→ Lösung S. 158

		true	false	not in the text
a)	Edinburgh Castle is a new building.	☐	☐	☐
b)	The Queen stays there when she visits Scotland.	☐	☐	☐
c)	The Castle is safe from attack.	☐	☐	☐
d)	The walls are very strong.	☐	☐	☐
e)	Today, very few people visit the Castle.	☐	☐	☐
f)	The One O'clock Gun was a kind of clock for ships.	☐	☐	☐
g)	The Edinburgh Tattoo takes place in winter.	☐	☐	☐
h)	It is very expensive to visit the Castle.	☐	☐	☐

Scanne den QR-Code und höre den Text an.

3. Für die Besucher des Edinburgh Castle gibt es einen elektronischen *Guide*. Hör die die Informationen an und beantworte die Fragen.

→ Lösung S. 158

a) You can listen to a guided tour in English, German, Spanish, Russian, and Mandarin. Which other languages can you choose?

____

b) How much do the guided tours cost?

____

c) How can you save time before you visit the Castle?

____

d) Is the "Historic Scotland Membership" pass only for Edinburgh Castle?

____

e) Where can you have afternoon tea?

____

f) Name three things you can buy in the gift shop.

____

g) Can you park at the Castle?

____

h) How can you get to the Castle without a car?

____

i) What time does the Castle close in December?

____

Scanne den QR-Code und höre den Text an.

4 Wegbeschreibungen (*Asking for and understanding directions*)

1. Du wirst am Bahnhof in deiner Stadt von Touristen auf Englisch angesprochen und nach dem Weg gefragt. Schreibe auf, wie du auf die Fragen antworten kannst.

→ Lösung S. 159

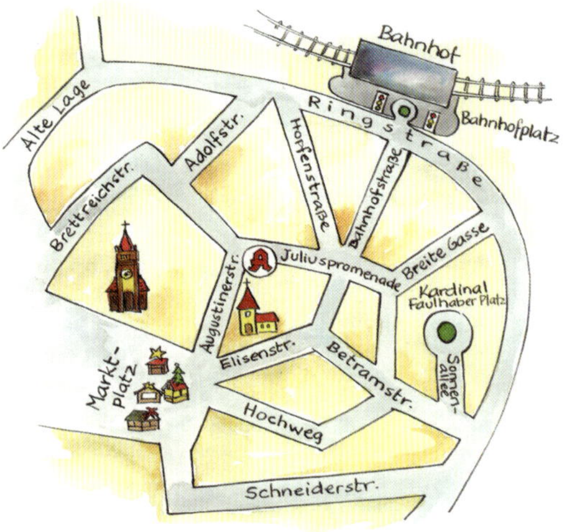

a) *Tourist 1*: I'm looking for a pharmacy. Can you help me?

You: Yes, of course. You ____________________

____

____

Tourist 1: ____________________

b) *Tourist 2*: Excuse me. Can you tell me how to get to the Marktplatz?

You: Yes, I can. ____________________

____

____

Tourist 2: ____________________

c) *Tourist 3*: I have to go Kardinal Faulhaber Platz. Can you tell me how to get there?

You: Yes, of course. ______________________

____

____

Tourist 3: ______________________

●○○ 2. Du bist in einer fremden Stadt angekommen und stehst auf dem Parkplatz, im Stadtplan oben links angezeigt. Höre die Wegbeschreibungen auf der Audiodatei an und markiere den beschriebenen Weg auf dem Plan.

5

→ Lösung S. 160

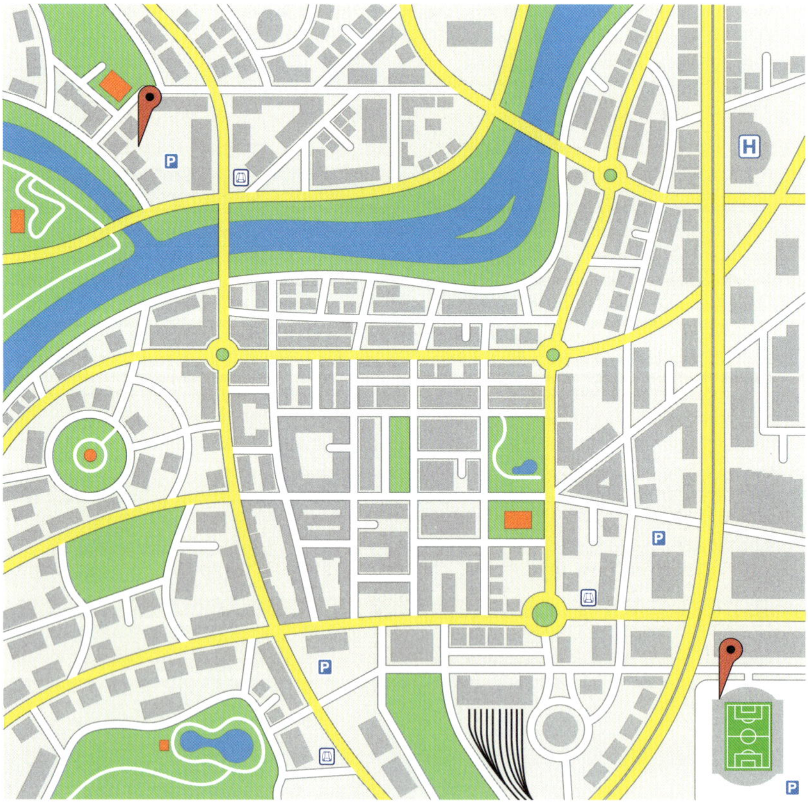

Scanne den QR-Code und höre den Text an.

1 Wortschatz: Verkehr und Verkehrsmittel (*Vocabulary: Traffic and transport*)

→ Übungen ab S. 148

1. a) If the last bus has left, we'll have to take a **taxi**. b) You can buy a **ticket** from the bus driver. c) A **ferry** is a boat that travels short distances, for example across a river. d) If you are in town all week, a **bus pass** is cheaper than buying a ticket every day. e) I would love to sail around the world in my own **boat**. f) Tower **Bridge** crosses the River Thames. g) A **tram** is a bit like a train that drives along the street.
   Lösungswort: **AIRPORT**

2. a) The train to Birmingham leaves from **platform** 4. b) Excuse me, does this **bus** go to the city centre? c) Catherine doesn't like travelling by **plane** because she's nervous about flying. d) They're building a new **tunnel** under the river. e) It was a very bad accident. Two people were flown to hospital by **helicopter**. f) We were late because there was a lot of **traffic**. g) Most big cities have **underground** trains. They are a fast way to travel around the city. h) We need to hurry to the **station**. Our train leaves in 10 minutes! i) This map is helpful if you want to tour the city on **foot**. j) Charlie rides his **bike** every day, even in bad weather.

3. a) bus pass b) underground train c) ticket machine d) public transport e) traffic lights f) train station g) Tube map h) northbound platform

4. a) What time does this train **arrive at** Paddington? b) Jack arrived late because he **got on** the wrong bus. c) Take the number 37 bus to the town hall and then **change** to the 63. d) How long have we been **waiting for** the tram? It's 20 minutes late! e) It was difficult to **get off** the train with my big suitcase. f) We had a great view of the city as we **drove over** the bridge.

5. a) Alex **takes** the train to school every day. / Alex **goes to school by train** every day. b) Linda **gets off** the bus two stops before me. c) Shall we go to town by bike or **on foot**? d) Please buy a **ticket** before you get on the train.

2 Eine Anzeige am Bahnhof verstehen (*Understanding station announcements*)

→ Übungen ab S. 151

1

1. a) The train now arriving at platform **3** is the 10.15 to London Paddington. b) The **15.20** to Bristol Temple Meads is now arriving at platform 5. The train stops at Swindon, **Bath** Spa and Bristol Temple Meads. c) Platform change: the 9.03 to Birmingham New Street will now leave from platform **9**, not platform **5**. d) The 17.46 to York will be **15** minutes late. We apologise for the late arrival of this service.

Scanne den QR-Code und höre den Text an.

2. Audio script:

   The 9.35 to Edinburgh will be late. This is because a tree has fallen onto the track. The next train to arrive at platform 4 will be the 9.42 to Manchester. At this time, we do not know when the Edinburgh train will arrive. If you are waiting for the 9.35 to Edinburgh, please go to the main hall and check the TV monitors for more information. We apologise to passengers waiting for this service.

   a) Nein, der Zug ist nicht pünktlich. b) Ein Baum ist auf die Gleise gefallen. c) Das weiß man noch nicht. d) Wir sollen in die Eingangshalle gehen und auf den Monitor schauen.

3 Sehenswürdigkeiten (*Sightseeing and attractions*)

→ Übungen ab S. 152

1. Audio script:

   Edinburgh Castle stands on Castle a) **Rock**. There has been a royal castle there since around the b) **12th** century. Kings and queens lived there until c) **1633**. After that, the Castle stopped being a home for royalty, but it was still important for the military. It was difficult to d) **attack** the Castle because it stands on a e) **hill**. Its walls are made of thick f) **stone**, which helped the Castle to survive hundreds of years of Scottish weather!

   Today, Edinburgh Castle is the most popular tourist g) **attraction** in Scotland. Around h) **1.5 million** people visit it every year. Visitors can take a guided tour or listen to information on i) **headphones** as they walk around. In some rooms, there are actors who bring the Castle's history to life.

   One of the biggest attractions at Edinburgh Castle is the j) **One O'clock** Gun. Every day, at 1 in the afternoon, a large gun is fired over the wall of the castle. This tradition started in 1861 and was done so that k) **ships** on the sea near Edinburgh would know the correct time. The Castle is also famous for the Edinburgh Military Tattoo, which is a performance by groups of military bands, mostly with pipes and drums. It takes place in l) **August** every year.

2. a) false b) not in the text c) true d) true e) false f) true g) false h) not in the text

3. Audio script:

   Hello and welcome to the Quick Visitor's Guide to Edinburgh Castle! If you are one of our many visitors from abroad, maybe you would like to listen to an audio guide in your own language? You can choose from English, French, German, Spanish, Italian, Japanese, Russian and Mandarin. Just put on the headphones, press "Play" and start listening! You can take one of our guided tours with a guide, who will tell you lots of interesting stories and answer all of your questions. These tours of the Castle are free. Just go to the meeting point at the Portcullis Gate.

Scanne den QR-Code und höre den Text an.

Do you hate waiting in long queues? Then save time and book your tickets online before you come. Visit our website for details. And if you want to come again, and visit other great attractions in Scotland too, why not buy a "Historic Scotland Membership" pass? You will save a lot of money and enjoy many interesting days out!
Feeling hungry? The Castle has some great places to eat! If you want a hot meal, the Redcoat Café is perfect. Try the delicious tomato soup! Or have one of our toasted sandwiches and a cup of hot chocolate. If you have time for a traditional afternoon tea, visit the Queen Anne Tea Room. There are homemade cakes, cookies, lots of different kinds of tea and coffee. You won't know what to choose!
If you are looking for a present, for yourself or a friend, there are lots of lovely things to buy in our gift shops. You will find clothes and jewellery hand-made in Scotland, and lots of fun presents for children. And did you know that Edinburgh Castle makes its own whisky? Of course, this is on sale at the gift shop too, along with shortbread, oatcakes and other traditional Scottish food.
Please note that visitors are not allowed to park directly outside the Castle. There is a car park near the Castle Rock: please park there and walk up the hill.
The Castle opens at 9.30 a.m. every day. It closes at 6 p.m. in summer and 5 p.m. in winter. Why not come early and spend the whole day with us? You won't be bored!

a) French, Italian or Japanese b) The guided tours are free. c) You can book your tickets online before you go. d) No, you can also visit other attractions with the pass. e) You can have afternoon tea in the Queen Anne Tea Room. f) You can buy clothes, jewellery, presents for children, whisky, shortbread, oatcakes and traditional Scottish food. (choose 3 of these). g) No, you can't. h) You can park near the Castle Rock and walk up the hill. i) It closes at 5 p.m.

4 Wegbeschreibungen (*Asking for and understanding directions*)

→ Übungen ab S. 155

1. Musterlösung:

a) *You*: Yes, of course. You cross Ringstrasse and go straight along Bahnhofstrasse until you get to Juliuspromenade. Then turn right and walk to the end of the road. You will see the pharmacy on the corner on your left.
Tourist 1: Thank you!

b) *You*: Yes, I can. Cross the road outside the station and walk straight along Bahnhofstrasse. Cross over Juliuspromenade and keep walking straight on. Turn right along Elisenstrasse and go past the church. You'll see the Marktplatz at the end of the road.
Tourist 2: Thank you for your help!

c) *You*: Yes, of course. When you leave the station, turn left and walk along Ringstrasse. Turn right when you get to Betramstrasse – it's the second road on your right. Then turn right again, into Sonnenallee, and walk to the end of the road. There is a little park there, and Kardinal Faulhaber Platz is just behind it.

Tourist 3: Thank you very much!

2. Audio script:

A: Excuse me, I need to get to the sports stadium. Can you help me?
B: The sports stadium? Yes, that's not too far from here. OK, what you need to do is go down to the small river, turn left and walk to the end of that road. Then turn left again and turn right at the first road you come to. You will cross the river here. After that, you have to walk straight on until you come to a roundabout.
A: A roundabout?
B: Yes, you know. Like a circle in the middle of the road.
A: Ah, I know what you mean! OK, what then?
B: You turn left at the first exit of the roundabout and walk straight on until you get to another roundabout. Then you turn right and walk straight on. After two or three minutes, there is another roundabout! You need to walk straight on here and leave the roundabout on the opposite side. Take the next road on the left and walk underneath the road bridge. You will see the sports stadium a few metres away on the other side of the bridge.
A: OK, I think I've got all that! Thank you for your help!
B: You're welcome!

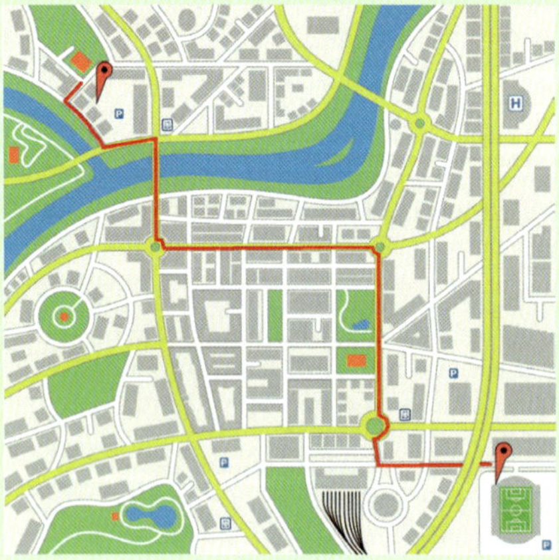

Scanne den QR-Code und höre den Text an.

Großbritannien: Geschichte und Traditionen (*Great Britain: History and traditions*)

1 Schottische Traditionen (*Scottish traditions*)

●○○ 1. Weißt du, wie diese typischen schottischen Sachen heißen? Schreibe den Namen unter die Bilder.

→ Lösung S. 168

a) ____________________

b) ____________________

c) ____________________

d) *The* ____________________

●○○ 2. Kreuze an, ob diese Aussagen richtig oder falsch sind.

→ Lösung S. 168

		true	false
a)	People dance at a ceilidh.	☐	☐
b)	The Edinburgh Fringe is a festival of Scottish food and drink.	☐	☐
c)	There are no dolphins near the coast of Scotland.	☐	☐
d)	A lot of Scottish men wear a kilt on their wedding day.	☐	☐
e)	You will often hear a pipe and drum band.	☐	☐
f)	Glasgow is the capital of Scotland.	☐	☐

3. Kennst du dich in Schottland aus?
Was wird hier beschrieben?

→ Lösung S. 168

Auld Lang Syne • Ben Nevis • haggis • Highland Games •
Loch Ness • Shetland Islands • shortbread

a) ____________________ is a famous lake where a mysterious monster lives, or so the story says.

b) ____________________ is a type of biscuit made with lots of butter and sugar.

c) The highest mountain in Britain can be found in the Scottish Highlands. Its name is ____________________ .

d) The ____________________ are part of Scotland, but are quite far north of the British Isles, in the North Sea.

e) New Year's Eve is always a big celebration in Scotland. At midnight, people hold hands and sing a song called ____________________ , which is about remembering old friends.

f) ____________________ is a special dish made of meat, vegetables and spices, which is cooked in a sheep's stomach.

g) ____________________ take place all over Scotland every summer. There is traditional music, dancing and food, and the chance for men to show how strong they are in different kinds of competitions.

4. Verbinde die Wörter, die zusammenpassen.

→ Lösung S. 168

a) play

your family tartan

haggis

d) eat

b) visit

Scots

Auld Lang Syne

e) speak

c) wear

Edinburgh

the bagpipes

f) sing

2 Das Leben in Wales (*Life in Wales*)

●○○ 1. Höre dir die Erzählung über Wales an und ergänze die fehlenden Wörter oder Zahlen.

→ Lösung S. 168

6

a) About ________________ people live in Wales.

b) The country has ________________ kilometres of coastline.

c) Wales has got a lot of hills and ________________ .

d) The highest mountain in the country is called ________________ .

e) The west coast is on the ________________ .

f) ________________ is the capital of Wales.

g) The capital city is unusual because it is on the ________________ .

h) The signs in Wales are in ________________ and ________________ .

i) About ________________ of Welsh people can speak the language.

j) You will find the most Welsh speakers in the ________________ of the country.

●●○ 2. Du kannst jetzt ein Interview mit einem Mädchen hören, dessen Eltern Waliser sind. Höre genau zu und kreuze die Aussagen an, die am besten zutreffen.

→ Lösung S. 169

7

a) Luke thinks that ________ .

- ☐ England is better than Wales
- ☐ England and Wales are not very different
- ☐ Wales is smaller than England

Scanne den QR-Code und höre den Text an.

b) Welsh people ______ .

- ☐ are happy if somebody thinks they are English
- ☐ do not enjoy speaking English
- ☐ think their culture is very special

c) When Caitlyn visits Wales ______ .

- ☐ she often gets in trouble
- ☐ her grandmother sometimes speaks to her in Welsh
- ☐ her brothers only speak Welsh

d) One thing Caitlyn likes about Wales is ______ .

- ☐ going to the beach
- ☐ visiting the cities
- ☐ walking in the mountains

e) In Wales, ______ .

- ☐ it always rains
- ☐ you shouldn't forget your warm jacket when you go out
- ☐ the weather is always hot and sunny

f) Rugby is ______ .

- ☐ a very popular sport in Wales
- ☐ quite boring to watch
- ☐ not as popular as football

g) Music and singing ______ .

- ☐ are only important for Welsh men
- ☐ are more popular than rugby
- ☐ are important in Welsh culture

3 Britische Geschichte (*British history*)

1. Kennst du dich in der britischen Geschichte aus?
Lies die Texte und ordne sie eine Epoche zu.
Gib auch an, welches Bild zu welcher Epoche gehört. → Lösung S. 170

British Empire • Elizabethan Age • Industrial Revolution • Norman Britain • Roman Britain • the Swinging Sixties

A

B

C

D

E

F

a) I'm twelve years old but I don't go to school. I have to work for 14 hours every day and I don't earn very much money. The machines in the factory are dangerous and people often hurt themselves. But what can I do? My family is poor and they need the money that I make from this job. The factory owners are the rich ones: they have a lot of money because people like us work so hard.

Epoche: ______________________________ Bild: ______

b) A few years ago, a big group of people arrived to live around here. We didn't like it much at first, but now life is pretty good. We have strong houses made of stone, good roads and even something called baths, which is a place to wash and has lots of hot water. Our houses are warm in winter and often have a nice floor made of mosaics. They speak a different language, but now we have started to use some of their words.

Epoche: ______________________________ Bild: ______

c) Britain is the best and most important country in the world! And the richest, too! We are rich because our factories make wonderful things for us to sell. And now there are British colonies all over the world, too. We send products from our colonies, like tea, back to Britain, and make even more money when we sell them. It's a good time to be British!

Epoche: ______________________________ Bild: ______

d) There is a queen on the English throne, and she wants to make England a powerful country in Europe. Sir Francis Drake has sailed to the New World and brought treasure home for the queen. And English is now the most important language in the country. There are a lot of new books in English, as well as new plays for the theatre. Here's a tip for a great evening out if you are in London: go to a new theatre called the Globe and see a play by a writer called William Shakespeare! I'm sure you'll enjoy it!

Epoche: ______________________________ Bild: ______

e) I just heard the news today: there's a new king! And he's not English at all – he's from France! Well, you know that Harold was the new king after King Edward died this year? Everything was fine until this William decided that he wants to be king! There was big fight down on the south coast, which people called the Battle of Hastings. And William won! So now the king and other important people don't even speak the same language as us – they speak French. I wish we could have a new English king instead of William.

Epoche: ______________________________ Bild: ______

f) Things are changing fast in Britain at the moment. World War 2 ended 20 years ago, and people have money to spend again. The young people are very different now. The women often wear very short skirts. Some men have long hair and wear colourful clothes. The songs they sing are about peace and love. And there is a new pop group called the Beatles who are making a new kind of music that the young people love.

Epoche: ______________________________ Bild: ______

4 Eine zeitübergreifende Geschichte schreiben (*Using the past perfect in a story*)

1. Lies die Stichworte über das Leben von William Shakespeare. Schreibe dann einen kurzen Text über die Ereignisse. In manchen Fällen brauchst du das *past perfect*, um auszudrücken, dass bestimmte Ereignisse vorher schon passiert sind. Verwende auch einige der Zeitwörter aus dem Kästchen, um die Satzteile zu verbinden. → Lösung S. 170

after	as soon as	because	then	so	when

- (be born) on 23rd April 1564 – (grow up) in Stratford-upon-Avon
- parents (move) there
- (marry) young – he (be) 18 – daughter (be born) the next year
- 10 years after – (leave) Stratford – (move) to London
- (work) for a theatre company – few years – (start) to write plays
- audiences never (see) such original, exciting plays before
- (write) some sad poems in 1596 – his son Hamnet (die) that year
- in 1599 his theatre company (build) the Globe Theatre
- (not have) a place to perform
- the company (build) a new Globe Theatre – old one (burn down)
- Shakespeare (die) in 1614 – (write) 37 plays

1 Schottische Traditionen (*Scottish traditions*)

→ Übungen ab S. 161

1. a) bagpipes b) kilt c) tartan d) The Highlands
2. a) true b) false c) false d) true e) true f) false
3. a) **Loch Ness** is a famous lake where a mysterious monster lives, or so the story says. b) **Shortbread** is a type of biscuit made with lots of butter and sugar. c) The highest mountain in Britain can be found in the Scottish Highlands. Its name is **Ben Nevis**. d) The **Shetland Islands** are part of Scotland, but are quite far north of the British Isles, in the North Sea. e) New Year's Eve is always a big celebration in Scotland. At midnight, people hold hands and sing a song called **Auld Lang Syne**, which is about remembering old friends. f) **Haggis** is a special dish made of meat, vegetables and spices, which is cooked in a sheep's stomach. g) **Highland Games** take place all over Scotland every summer. There is traditional music, dancing and food, and the chance for men to show how strong they are in different kinds of competitions.
4. a) play the bagpipes b) visit Edinburgh c) wear your family tartan d) eat haggis e) speak Scots f) sing Auld Lang Syne

2 Das Leben in Wales (*Life in Wales*)

→ Übungen ab S. 163

6

1. Audio script:

Hello again, and welcome to our 5-minute fact files! Today I'm going to tell you some interesting facts about Wales. Wales is a small country in the west of the UK. It has a population of about 3.15 million. It is a beautiful country with 2704 kilometres of coastline, and a lot of hills and mountains. The highest mountain is called Snowdon, which is 1085 metres high. The west coast of Wales is on the Irish Sea: if you swim towards the west, you will end up in Ireland!
The capital city of Wales is Cardiff, which is very popular with tourists. As well as the old castle, there are lots of interesting museums to enjoy. The city also has a lot of parks and green spaces, so it is a great place to spend time outside. It is directly on the coast, which is unusual for a capital city! One thing you will notice when you visit Wales is that all of the signs are in two languages, English and Welsh. This can seem a little strange at first if you have just arrived from England, but the Welsh language is an important part of the country's culture. Around 20 % of the population can speak it. The most Welsh speakers are from the north-west of the country, where many people still speak it as their first language.

a) About **3.15 million** people live in Wales. b) The country has **2,704** kilometres of coastline. c) Wales has got a lot of hills and **mountains**. d) The highest mountain in the country is called **Snowden**. e) The west coast is on the **Irish Sea**. f) **Cardiff** is the capital of Wales. g) The capital city is unusual because it is on the **coast**. h) The signs in Wales are in **English** and **Welsh**. i) About **20 %** of Welsh people can speak the language. j) You will find the most Welsh speakers in the **north-west** of the country.

Scanne den QR-Code und höre den Text an.

2. Audio script:

Luke: Hi, everyone! Thanks for listening to our new podcast about pupils here at Greenvale School with parents from another country. Today we're talking to Caitlyn, whose parents are from Wales. But come on, Caitlyn, Wales is more or less the same as England, isn't it? Are the two countries really that different?

Caitlyn: Hey, Luke, don't say that to someone from Wales! Welsh people are very proud of their country, culture and, of course, language!

Luke: I hear that Welsh is difficult to learn. Can you speak it?

Caitlyn: No, not really. I understand a few words, but my parents don't really speak it either. But sometimes my grandma shouts at me and my brothers in Welsh if we do something bad! So, when she speaks Welsh, I know that I'm in trouble!

Luke: (*laughs*) That's funny! So anyway, I guess you go to Wales quite often, do you?

Caitlyn: Yes, three or four times a year, to visit our family.

Luke: So, what do you like best about the country?

Caitlyn: Well, for one thing, there are some beautiful beaches. We live in the city, so when we go to Wales it's great to go out and spend time on the beach every day.

Luke: But isn't Wales a bit cold for a beach holiday? It rains every day, doesn't it?

Caitlyn: No, it doesn't! We have great weather there ... well, some of the time. OK, it's true that you should probably take a warm jacket with you. But that's one thing that makes it special: you come home after a long, cold walk on the beach and warm up with a cup of hot chocolate. Delicious!

Luke: Hmm, I'm not so sure. I think I still prefer beaches in warm countries ... But OK, what about sport? I hear that Welsh people aren't really big football fans, right?

Caitlyn: Oh, people like football, but the big sport here is rugby! Rugby is a very exciting team sport, with lots of action. And the Welsh national team is very good! And you should hear the fans in the stadium when Wales are playing! They don't only shout; they sing, too! Music is another big part of Welsh culture, and the people love singing. There are a lot of choirs just for men, and the singing is really beautiful.

Luke: That's interesting. Now, there's something else I'd like to know. Why is there a dragon on the Welsh flag?

Caitlyn: Well, that's an interesting story ....

a) Luke thinks that **England and Wales are not very different**. b) Welsh people think **that their culture is very special**. c) When Caitlyn visits Wales **her grandmother sometimes speaks to her in Welsh**. d) One thing Caitlyn likes about Wales is **going to the beach**. e) In Wales, **you shouldn't forget your warm jacket when you go out**. f) Rugby is **a very popular sport in Wales**. g) Music and singing are **important in Welsh culture**.

Scanne den QR-Code und höre den Text an.

3 Britische Geschichte (*British history*)

→ Übungen ab S. 165

1. a) Industrial Revolution, F b) Roman Britain, D c) British Empire, B d) Elizabethan Age, A e) Norman Britain, C f) the Swinging Sixties, E

4 Eine zeitübergreifende Geschichte schreiben (*Using the past perfect in a story*)

→ Übungen ab S. 167

1. Musterlösung:

   William Shakespeare was born on 23rd April 1564 and grew up in Stratford-upon-Avon after his parents had moved there. He married young, when he was 18, and his first daughter was born the next year. Ten years after he had married, he left Stratford and moved to London. He had worked for a theatre company for a few years when he started to write plays for the company to perform. Audiences had never seen such original, exciting plays before. He wrote some very sad poems in 1596 because his son Hamnet had died that year. In 1599 his theatre company built the Globe Theatre because they did not have a place to perform. They had to build a new Globe in 1614 because the old one had burnt down. When Shakespeare died in 1614, he had written 37 plays.

Sport (*Sport*)

1 Wortschatz: Sport (*Vocabulary: Sport*)

●○○ 1. Finde 10 verschiedene Sportarten. → Lösung S. 177

M	N	C	Y	C	L	I	N	G
P	A	R	E	R	K	L	Z	O
S	W	I	M	M	I	N	G	L
K	W	C	A	N	C	S	B	F
I	A	K	R	O	W	I	N	G
I	P	E	A	U	A	R	S	P
N	D	T	T	E	N	N	I	S
G	V	H	H	O	C	K	E	Y
J	U	D	O	Q	U	C	L	F
E	E	S	N	G	J	A	O	L

●○○ 2. Füge das richtige Wort in den Sätzen ein. → Lösung S. 177

fouls • goalkeeper • helmet • pitch • red card

a) The referee showed Bale a ____________________ and sent him off.

b) The ____________________ was so wet after all the rain that the players couldn't stop falling over.

c) That team is very aggressive. There are always a lot of ____________________ when they play.

d) We didn't win because the other team's ____________________ made a great save at the last minute!

e) It's a good idea to wear a ____________________ for some sports to protect your head.

●○○ 3. Kannst du die Wörter entziffern, die mit Sport zu tun haben? → Lösung S. 177

a) I'm quite good at skiing now. I went down the black i k s o p l s e for the first time this year!

b) If you go on a lot of long bike rides, it's a good idea to have a comfortable d e l s a d to sit on.

c) The s f n a started singing when their team came onto the t p i h c.

d) We couldn't believe it when Kane missed the y p t e l n a!

e) The Cup Final is taking place at Wembley d a S u m i t.

f) Many e a t l e s h t dream of winning a medal at the Olympic Games.

g) a v l o l e l y b l is my favourite team sport. You have to hit the ball over a net with your hands or arms.

h) Frank couldn't come swimming with us because he'd forgotten his s t u r k n.

●○○ 4. Wähle das Wort, das am besten in den Sätzen passt. → Lösung S. 177

a) Football players wear ______ to protect their legs.
☐ helmets ☐ long socks ☐ shin pads

b) The ______ blew her whistle to start the game.
☐ fan ☐ referee ☐ manager

c) Tennis is played with a ______ and a ball.
☐ racket ☐ hitter ☐ bat

d) The athletics team trains on the running ______ on Friday afternoons.
☐ place ☐ track ☐ pitch

e) In our last hockey match, the final ______ was 3-0 to us.
☐ result ☐ points ☐ score

2 Internationale Sportsveranstaltungen (*International sporting events*)

●○○ 1. Jeder Absatz des Textes soll eine Überschrift erhalten. Entscheide, welche jeweils am besten passt. Eine Überschrift brauchst du nicht.

→ Lösung S. 177

More cash needed — title for: ________

The best fans are quiet fans! — title for: ________

A different kind of Olympics — title for: ________

Why training is difficult — title for: ________

What athletes want — title for: ________

The Paralympic Games

a) Everybody knows the Olympic Games. People all around the world enjoy watching this sporting event, which takes place every four years. But a couple of weeks after the Olympics comes another sporting event that has also become very popular: the Paralympics.

b) The Paralympic Games are for people who are disabled. All kinds of different people can take part: for example, some are in wheelchairs, some have lost part or all of an arm or leg, and others are blind. This is the big difference between Paralympic athletes and the sportsmen and women who take part in the Olympics. But all of these athletes are the same in three important ways: they love their sport, they train hard and they want to be the best!

c) Some of the sports at the Paralympics are different versions of the ones non-disabled athletes do. For example, people race around the running tracks in wheelchairs, or they might have special legs made of metal. Blind athletes run with a guide, who, of course, also has to be fast! However, there are other sports that we don't see every day. One of them is goalball. This is played by people who cannot see well. The players wear masks on their eyes, and have to roll the ball into the goal. There are bells inside the ball to help the players know where it is. This means that the fans are not allowed to shout or sing during the game!

d) Money is a problem for many disabled athletes. It is expensive to do a sport to a very high level, but it is more difficult for disabled people to find sponsors. One reason for this is that many people do not know much about disabled sport and do not watch it on TV or go to events. However, the Paralympic Games are changing this, with more people watching every time. This might be because the Paralympics show what people can do, not what they can't do. And they can do great things!

●●○ 2. Lies den Text noch einmal und beantworte die folgenden Fragen dazu.

→ Lösung S. 178

a) How often do the Olympic Games take place?

____

b) Do Paralympic athletes need to be in a wheelchair?

____

c) In what ways are Paralympic athletes the same as Olympic athletes?

____

d) How do blind runners find their way around the running track?

____

e) What kind of people play goalball?

____

f) Why are noisy fans a bad thing at a goalball match?

____

g) Why do disabled athletes have less money than other sportspeople?

____

3 Ein Unfallbericht (*Writing an accident report*)

1. Ein Austauschschüler bei dir an der Schule hat während des Sportunterrichts einen Unfall gehabt. Der Sportlehrer hat ein Formular über den Unfall ausgefüllt, aber der Schüler bittet dich, einen Bericht für ihn auf Englisch zu verfassen. Lies zuerst den Bericht des Sportlehrers, darüber, was passiert ist. → Lösung S. 178

St. Josef Schule – Unfallformular	
Datum:	27. Oktober 2016
Uhrzeit des Unfalls:	ca. 10.15 Uhr
Unfallort:	Turnhalle der St. Josef Schule
Anwesende Lehrkraft:	Herr Mayer
Name des Schülers:	Simon Matthews
Ablauf des Unfalls:	Während eines Volleyballspiels wurde der Schüler mit dem Ball am Kopf getroffen. Er fiel zu Boden und lag zunächst bewegungslos. Nach ungefähr eine Minute kam der Schüler wieder zu sich. Er klagte über starke Kopfschmerzen.
Weitere Maßnahmen:	Der Schüler bekam eine Kühlkompresse für seinen Kopf. Obwohl es ihm schnell wieder gut ging, wurde vorsichtshalber der Notarzt gerufen. Der Schüler musste nicht ins Krankenhaus, wurde aber für den Rest des Tages nach Hause geschickt, er soll sich ausruhen.

●○○ 2. Schreib aus den Notizen einen Bericht auf Englisch. Denk daran, es geht nicht darum, eine Übersetzung zu erfassen, sondern die Bedeutung des deutschen Textes zu übertragen. Überlege also, was eigentlich passiert ist und mache dir ein paar Notizen auf Englisch, bevor du den Bericht schreibst. Die angegebenen Wörter werden dir ein paar Ideen geben. → Lösung S. 178

play • hit • head • fall • not move • wake up • headache • cold • doctor • home • rest

Simon was playing volleyball – Ball hit his head …

●●○ 3. Schreibe nun den Bericht in ganzen Sätzen. → Lösung S. 178

1 Wortschatz: Sport (*Vocabulary: Sport*)

→ Übungen ab S. 171

1.

M	N	**C**	**Y**	**C**	**L**	**I**	**N**	**G**
P	A	**R**	E	R	K	L	Z	**O**
S	**W**	**I**	**M**	**M**	**I**	**N**	**G**	**L**
K	W	**C**	**A**	N	C	S	B	**F**
I	A	**K**	**R**	**O**	**W**	**I**	**N**	**G**
I	P	**E**	**A**	U	A	R	S	P
N	D	**T**	**T**	**E**	**N**	**N**	**I**	**S**
G	V	H	**H**	**O**	**C**	**K**	**E**	**Y**
J	**U**	**D**	**O**	Q	U	C	L	F
E	E	S	**N**	G	J	A	O	L

cycling, swimming, rowing, tennis, hockey, judo, skiing, cricket, marathon, golf

2. a) The referee showed Bale a **red card** and sent him off. b) The **pitch** was so wet after all the rain that the players couldn't stop falling over. c) That team is very aggressive. There are always a lot of **fouls** when they play. d) We didn't win because the other team's **goalkeeper** made a great save at the last minute! e) It's a good idea to wear a **helmet** for some sports to protect your head.

3. a) I'm quite good at skiing now. I went down the black **ski slope** for the first time this year! b) If you go on a lot of long bike rides, it's a good idea to have a comfortable **saddle** to sit on. c) The **fans** started singing when their team came onto the **pitch**. d) We couldn't believe it when Kane missed the **penalty**! e) The Cup Final is taking place at Wembley **Stadium**. f) Many **athletes** dream of winning a medal at the Olympic Games. g) **Volleyball** is my favourite team sport. You have to hit the ball over a net with your hands or arms. h) Frank couldn't come swimming with us because he'd forgotten his **trunks**.

4. a) Football players wear **shin pads** to protect their legs. b) The **referee** blew her whistle to start the game. c) Tennis is played with a **racket** and a ball. d) The athletics team trains on the running **track** on Friday afternoons. e) In our last hockey match, the final **score** was 3-0 to us.

2 Internationale Sportveranstaltungen (*International sporting events*)

→ Übungen ab S. 173

1. a) A different kind of Olympics b) What athletes want c) The best fans are quiet fans! d) More cash needed

2. Musterlösung

a) The Olympic Games take place every four years. b) No, they don't. Some are in a wheelchair, but others have lost an arm or leg, or are blind. c) All athletes love their sport, train hard and want to be the best. d) Blind runners have a guide who runs with them. e) People who cannot see play goalball. f) If the fans are noisy, the players cannot hear the bells inside the ball. g) It is more difficult for disabled athletes to find sponsors, because disabled sport is not as popular as other types of sport.

3 Ein Unfallbericht (*Writing an accident report*)

→ Übungen ab S. 175

2. Musterlösung:

Simon was playing volleyball; ball hit his head; fell down; not moving; woke up with a headache; something cold on his head; doctor came; sent him home to rest

3. Musterlösung

On 27th October Simon Matthews had an accident in the gym at St Josef's School. It happened in the morning sport lesson. While we were playing volleyball, a ball hit Simon on the head. He fell down and for a minute he was lying on the floor, but he was not moving. Then he woke up and said he had a bad headache.
Our sports teacher, Mr Mayer, brought something cold to put on Simon's head. Then he called the doctor to make sure that there was nothing wrong with Simon's head. The doctor came and checked him. He said Simon didn't have to go to hospital, but should go home and rest.

Die Medien (*The media*)

1 Wortschatz: Elektronische Medien (*Vocabulary: Electronic media*)

●○○ 1. Was kann man mit elektronischen Medien alles machen? Vervollständige die Wörter in diesen Sätzen. → Lösung S. 190

downloaded • e-card • instant • internet • social networking

a) Christina ____________________ some songs to listen to on her phone.

b) I surf the ____________________ for at least an hour every day.

c) When I don't have time to talk, I send my friends an ____________________ message.

d) Tom never sends paper Christmas cards any more. Instead, his friends and family get an ____________________ from him.

e) How much time do you spend on ____________________ ____________________ websites?

●○○ 2. Wähle das Verb, das in diesen Sätzen am besten passt. → Lösung S. 190

a) Do you make / take / do a lot of photos with your phone?

b) They made / took / did a video of the concert and posted it on the school website.

c) We often chat / post / visit online with our cousins in Florida.

d) Stop watching / making / playing video games and do your homework!

e) Hannah has made / sent / downloaded me about 10 messages in the last hour but I haven't answered her yet.

f) She often visits / downloads / watches her favourite singer's fan site.

●○○ 3. Wenn wir eine SMS schreiben, verwenden wir oft Kurzformen. Verbinde diese Abkürzungen mit ihrer Bedeutung. → Lösung S. 190

a) LOL	tonight
b) CU	you are
c) 2nite	thank you
d) OMG	laughing out loud
e) B4	see you
f) UR	OK
g) K	before
h) TY	oh my God

●●○ 4. Jetzt lies diese Kurznachrichten und schreibe auf, wie sie „richtig“ heißen sollen. → Lösung S. 190

a)

____

____

____

b)

____

____

____

c)

____

____

____

5. Um was für eine Art Medien geht es? Lies die Beschreibungen in dieser Übung und entscheide, welches Medium beschrieben wird.

→ Lösung S. 190

a) This is a pretty old type of media. A lot of people think it's boring because you can't actually watch anything on it, but that's why I like it. You don't have to look at a screen, but you can listen to music or news reports while you're doing something else. My dad always uses it in the car, and I like to turn it on before I start my homework. I like hearing voices in the background while I work.

____

b) My mum calls me a couch potato. Well, maybe I am, especially at the weekend! But this is my favourite way to relax. I don't have to think: I can just sit there and enjoy my favourite shows. If my brother's there too, we always fight over the remote control because we both want to choose what to watch. And yes, OK, some of the shows are pretty bad. But you can learn a lot, too. I love travel shows, for example – finding out about amazing places that I will probably never visit!

____

c) I'm sorry, but this is the one thing in my life I can't live without! I take it with me everywhere and start to feel nervous if I don't have a connection. My whole life is in this small machine: phone numbers, e-mails, dates. And I can't imagine what I would do if I had to wait somewhere, for example at the bus stop or at the doctor's, and I didn't have it with me. It's so boring if you're sitting around and can't even watch a video.

____

d) This electronic product is amazing. How did people work before it was invented? I can use it to write school projects, to look up things on the internet, read articles and play games. OK, I can't just put it in my pocket when I go out, but it still has everything I need.

____

2 Was ist das für ein Buch? (*What kind of book is it?*)

1. Es gibt natürlich viele verschiedene Arten von Büchern und Filmen. Aber wie heißen die verschiedenen Kategorien auf Englisch? Finde die Begriffe, die zu den Beschreibungen passen.

→ Lösung S. 190

action • biography • comedy • love story • science fiction • thriller

a) This type of book or film is very exciting! There is a lot of action, and some of the characters are usually killed. It is also scary because you never know what is going to happen next.

____

b) A book or film about a real person's life, often a famous person like a film star, is called a

____________________ .

c) This book or film is not about real life, but is about things that might happen! It is often about the future, or about life in space. In many examples, the characters meet "people" from other planets.

____

d) If you like laughing a lot, then this is the kind of story for you!

____

e) One thing you can say about ____________________ films is that they are never boring! There is always a lot to see: cars driving very fast (and often crashing), people running around, shooting guns, even jumping out of planes!

f) It's one of the oldest kinds of story in the world. Two people meet. Sometimes they like each other from the start, but they often hate each other at first, or have some problems with each other. But, in the end, they always see that they are perfect for each other and there is a happy ending!

____

2. Vier Personen wollen ins Kino gehen.
Lies die Personenbeschreibungen und entscheide, was für einen Film jede/r anschauen sollte.

→ Lösung S. 190

a) Tom is a real romantic at heart. He likes films about people, but doesn't enjoy stories that are violent or aggressive. He wants a film to make him feel good! He's seeing his new girlfriend this weekend and would like a film that they can watch together.

Tom should watch a ______________________ .

b) Rosie wants to travel to another world when she goes to the cinema, maybe even another planet. She often thinks about what our world could be like 100 years from now. And if she had the chance to take a trip on a space ship, she would definitely go!

Rosie should watch a ______________________ film.

c) When Sam watches a film, he doesn't want to feel nervous or scared, or even excited. All he wants is good entertainment. "Too many bad things happen in the world," he says. "When I go to the cinema, I want to forget about them for an hour or two."

Sam should watch a ______________________ .

d) Christina likes exciting stories that surprise her, or even shock her. She loves watching characters go into an old, dark house, where they might meet a killer or a ghost. When she watches a film, she wants to feel her heart beating very hard!

Christina should watch a ______________________ .

3 Zeitschriften für Teenager (*Teen magazines*)

●○○ 1. Welcher Artikel in deiner Zeitschrift gehört in welche Rubrik? → Lösung S. 190

celebrity news • fashion • health and beauty • music • problem page • relationships

Type of article	Description
a)	You can ask a question, for example if you and your best friend have had a big argument, or you think your parents don't understand you. You will get some advice about what to do.
b)	Read about the latest clothes and how to get the look
c)	Read about how to tell a boy or girl that you like them, or romantic things to do with your boyfriend or girlfriend
d)	Read all about your favourite actors or other stars
e)	Find out about different singers and bands: their latest CD, when their next concert will be or the meaning of their new song
f)	Get tips on fitness, what to eat and drink, the latest make-up and so on

●○○ 2. Unten findest du einen Leserbrief aus der *problem page* einer Teenager-Zeitschrift und die Antwort darauf. Einige Satzteile wurden aus den Texten herausgenommen. Setze sie an den richtigen Stellen wieder ein. Eins davon brauchst du nicht. → Lösung S. 190

Dear Angie,

I've got a big problem at home. I have a smart phone but my parents won't let me use it all the time when I'm at home. I have to put it in the kitchen when I get home and leave it there a) ____________________ . Then I'm allowed to have it for about 30 minutes, but b) ____ until the next morning.

I don't think this is fair! All my friends are allowed to have their phones for as long as they like. I am missing a lot of messages in my class chat group and I can't talk about them the next day at school.
As well as this, c) ________________________________ , not just chatting. I want to download music and watch videos, too, but 30 minutes isn't enough time. Even at the weekend, I'm only allowed to have the phone d) ________________________________ .
I have lots of hobbies and I would not spend all day just playing with the phone. How can I ask my parents let me use the phone for longer than 30 minutes?
Ellie

Dear Ellie,
I understand why you are upset, but you need to understand your parents, too. They want you to do well at school and e) ________________________________ . Maybe they are worried that you would spend all your free time playing on the phone. But I agree that 30 minutes a day is not very much time. It is important f) ________________________________ (calmly and politely!) and explain why you would like more time with the phone. Offer to do g) ________________________________ in exchange for more phone time. This will show them that you don't just want to sit on the sofa all day with your phone! You could also suggest trying longer phone times for, say, one month. If your parents are happy with the way you use the phone during that time, they will probably let you use your phone for longer. Good luck!

The missing phrases:
- after that my mum takes it away
- for quite a short time
- I want to use my phone for other things
- to talk to your parents
- because my friends are allowed to
- some extra jobs around the house
- until I've finished my homework
- concentrate on your homework

4 Nachrichten verstehen: ein Radiobericht (*Understanding a radio report*)

●○○ 1. Ergänze diese Sätze mit den richtigen Begriffen. → Lösung S. 191

breakfast show • call-in show • news • presenter • sports report

a) A ____________________ is a person who leads a discussion and introduces guests on a radio show.

b) A radio ____________________ is a programme in which listeners can phone the radio station and take part in the discussion.

c) Most radio stations have a ____________________ early in the morning. They play music and talk about things happening in the world that day.

d) If you want to hear the latest football results, listen to the ____________________ .

e) People all around the world listen to the BBC World Service because they know the ____________________ they hear is neutral and correct.

●○○ 2. Du hörst eine Nachrichtensendung im Radio. Kreuze an, was richtig ist. → Lösung S. 191

8

a) You are listening to the news at ______ .

☐ 6 o'clock in the morning ☐ 6 o'clock in the evening

b) ______ were stolen from the car.

☐ A computer and a phone ☐ A laptop and a bag

c) The things were stolen ______ .

☐ after 7 p.m. ☐ after 9 p.m.

d) Mrs Monk's dog is called ______ .

☐ Simon ☐ Benjy

Scanne den QR-Code und höre den Text an.

e) Mr Tobin saw the dog in the river because ______ .

☐ he was also swimming there ☐ he was jogging nearby

f) More than ______ fans went to see the football match.

☐ five thousand ☐ nine thousand

g) ______ scored the first goal for Oxford United.

☐ Michael Johnson ☐ Martin O'Connor

h) The weather in Didcot tomorrow will be ______ .

☐ cold and rainy ☐ sunny and windy.

●●○ 3. Höre dir die Sendung nochmal an und korrigiere die Aussagen.

8

→ Lösung S. 192

a) The thief opened the car door to steal the computer.

____

b) Simon Tobin doesn't like dogs.

____

c) Benjy the dog died while he was in the river.

____

d) A player from Didcot Town got a red card.

____

e) Didcot won the match.

____

____

f) It is going to rain all day in Didcot tomorrow.

____

____

Scanne den QR-Code und höre den Text an.

5 Einen Zeitungsartikel schreiben (*Writing a newspaper article*)

1. Zwei Jungen aus deiner Klasse sind verletzt worden, während sie ein Spiel mit ihren Handys gespielt haben. Du schreibst darüber für die Schülerzeitung einen Artikel. Lies zuerst die Notizen und schreibe dann den Artikel. Überlege zuerst, in welcher Reihenfolge du die Informationen sortierst.

→ Lösung S. 192

more interesting details • background information • headline • basic information: who / what / where / when / why

two boys from Staunton Road School / hospital / playing a game on their phones / Leo Jackson and Alex Burns playing "Catch the Dragon" / walked in front of a car / driver Caroline Duncan could not stop / hit boys with car / not driving fast / boys not badly hurt / taken to hospital; went home in the evening / Ms Duncan: not hurt but had a shock / Catch the Dragon: virtual game / "catch" dragons and other figures on phones / fans: better than normal computer games: have to go out and walk around / accident shows: game can be dangerous / police officer Mark Bryson: "Do not walk around with eyes on phone, especially near a road / boys were OK; you might not be / do not play on the street" / information about safe places to play: catch-a-dragon.com

6 Werbung (*Advertising*)

1. Du hast eine neue Zeitschrift für Teenager entdeckt. Sie heißt "Teen Talk". Du möchtest eine Werbung dafür in deiner Schülerzeitung veröffentlichen. Lies die Informationen über die Zeitschrift und schreibe einen Werbeartikel darüber.

→ Lösung S. 192

Product information:

What is it?	teen magazine
What is it called?	Teen Talk
Who is it for?	girls and boys
Why is it special?	Not just fashion and girlfriend / boyfriend problems: music news; technology corner; nature; teenagers doing unusual things
How much does it cost?	£ 2.50

Useful words:

buy • discover • exciting • famous • find out • fun • great • new • popular • read

1 Wortschatz: Elektronische Medien (*Vocabulary: Electronic media*)

→ Übungen ab S. 179

1. a) Christina **downloaded** some songs to listen to on her phone. b) I surf the **internet** for at least an hour every day. c) When I don't have time to talk, I send my friends an **instant** message. d) Tom never sends paper Christmas cards any more. Instead, his friends and family get an **e-card** from him. e) How much time do you spend on **social networking** websites?

2. a) Do you **take** a lot of photos with your phone? b) They **made** a video of the concert and posted it on the school website. c) We often **chat** online with our cousins in Florida. d) Stop **playing** video games and do your homework! e) Hannah has **sent** me about 10 messages in the last hour but I haven't answered her yet. f) She often **visits** her favourite singer's fan site.

3. a) LOL: laughing out loud b) CU: see you c) 2nite: tonight d) OMG: oh my God e) B4: before f) UR: you are g) K: OK h) TY: thank you

4. a) Are you going to Clare's party tonight? See you later! b) What did you tell Joe about me? We need to talk! c) Oh my God! I want to see that video! Please send me the link!!!

5. a) radio b) television c) mobile phone d) laptop/computer

2 Was ist das für ein Buch? (*What kind of book is this?*)

→ Übungen ab S. 182

1. a) thriller b) biography c) science fiction d) comedy e) action f) love story

2. a) love story b) science fiction c) comedy d) thriller

3 Zeitschriften für Teenager (*Teen magazines*)

→ Übungen ab S. 184

1. a) problem page b) fashion c) relationships d) celebrity news e) music f) health and beauty

2. a) until I've finished my homework b) after that my mum takes it away c) I want to use my phone for other things d) for quite a short time e) concentrate on your homework f) to talk to your parents g) some extra jobs around the house
   Extra phrase: because my friends are allowed to

4 Nachrichten verstehen: ein Radiobericht (*Understanding a radio report*)

→ Übungen ab S. 186

1. a) A **presenter** is a person who leads a discussion and introduces guests on a radio show. b) A radio **call-in show** is a programme in which listeners can phone the radio station and take part in the discussion. c) Most radio stations have a **breakfast show** early in the morning. They play music and talk about things happening in the world that day. d) If you want to hear the latest football results, listen to the **sports report**. e) People all around the world listen to the BBC World Service because they know the **news** they hear is neutral and correct.

8

2. Audio script:

You're listening to Radio Didcot. It's 6 p.m. on Thursday, the 25th of October and here is your local news with Paul Miller.
Paul Miller: Good evening. Police are looking for a thief who stole a laptop and smartphone from a car parked on Abingdon Road last night. The car window was broken and the computer and phone were taken from the back seat. The police are asking anyone who was in Abingdon Road between 7 and 9 p.m. last night to call them on 01235 96803 if they saw anything.
This afternoon, local man Simon Tobin was given a medal by the Didcot Dogs and Cats Club, because he rescued a dog from the river. Last June, Mrs Winnie Monk was walking her dog, Benjy, by the river. Benjy jumped in for a swim but the water was moving very fast that day and he couldn't climb out again. Mr Tobin, who was jogging along the same path, saw what happened and jumped in to save Benjy. He caught the dog and got him out of the river. Afterwards, Mr Tobin said: "I love dogs, so it was clear that I had to jump in. I couldn't let him die. It's great to get this medal today, but I'm just happy that everything was OK!" Mrs Monk said Simon Tobin was a real hero and that she would never forget him.
Didcot Town football club had a big match this afternoon against Oxford United. More than 5000 fans travelled to Oxford's Kassam Stadium to cheer for their team. Didcot started well but Michael Johnson scored for Oxford at the end of the first half. In the second half, David Smith got a red card for a foul on Didcot's Martin O'Connor. But even with only ten men, Oxford were too good for the visitors. They scored another goal just before the end of the match to win 2-0.

The weather tomorrow in Didcot will be sunny but very windy. The temperature will be around 12° Celsius but it will feel colder. There is a chance of rain in the early evening.

a) You are listening to the news at **6 o'clock in the evening**. b) **A computer and a phone** were stolen from the car. c) The things were stolen **after 7 p.m.** d) Mrs Monk's dog is called **Benjy**. e) Mr Tobin saw the dog in the river because **he was jogging nearby**. f) More than **five thousand** fans went to see the football match. g) **Michael Johnson** scored first for Oxford United. h) The weather in Didcot tomorrow will be **sunny and windy**.

Scanne den QR-Code und höre den Text an.

3. a) The thief broke the car window to steal the computer. b) Simon Tobin loves dogs. c) Benjy the dog didn't die while he was in the river / Benjy the dog was rescued from the river. d) A player from Oxford United got a red card. e) Didcot lost the match. f) It might rain in the evening tomorrow.

5 Einen Zeitungsartikel schreiben (*Writing a newspaper article*)

→ Übungen ab S. 188

1. Musterlösung:

Mobile phone game ends in hospital
Two boys from Staunton Road School ended up in hospital yesterday because they were playing a virtual game on their phones. The boys, Leo Jackson and Alex Burns, were playing "Catch the Dragon", when they stepped out onto the road in front of a car. The driver, Caroline Duncan, was not able to stop in time and hit the boys with her car. Luckily, she was not driving very fast, so the boys were not badly hurt. They were taken to hospital but were allowed to go home in the evening. Ms Duncan was not hurt in the accident but had a bad shock.
"Catch the Dragon" is a virtual game in which people have to "catch" dragons and other figures virtually with their phones. Fans say it is better than a normal computer game, because players have to leave the house and walk around instead of sitting at home in front of a screen. However, this accident shows that the game can be dangerous.
Police officer Mark Bryson warned: "Please do not walk around with your eyes on your phone, especially near a road. These two boys were OK, but you might not be so lucky. We advise people not to play this game on the street."
If you want information about safe places to play the game, visit catch-a-dragon.com.

6 Werbung (*Advertising*)

→ Übungen ab S. 189

1. Musterlösung:

Teen Talk – the great new magazine for young people!
Are you bored of the normal teen magazines about fashion and problems with your boyfriend? Are you interested in topics for girls and boys? Then here's a great new magazine for you!
Teen Talk: read about new music, discover the latest technology, read stories about teenagers doing unusual things!
Teen Talk: the exciting new magazine for things you really care about!
Only £ 2.50 – buy your copy today!

Reisen (*Travelling*)

1 Wortschatz: Bei einer Gastfamilie (*Vocabulary: Staying with a host family*)

●○○ 1. Wie heißen diese Alltagsgegenstände auf Englisch?
Fülle das Wortgitter aus und finde das Lösungswort. → Lösung S. 203

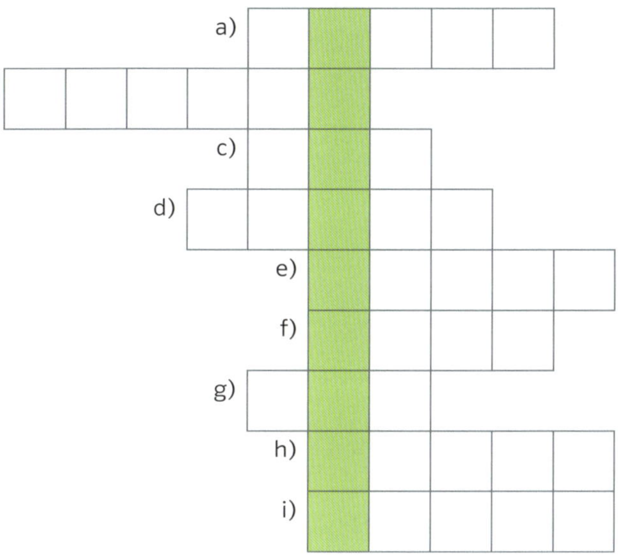

Lösungswort:

a) We eat cereal or soup from this.

b) Put this on your bread.

c) The British drink a lot of ________ .

d) We serve food on a ________ .

e) We cut our food with this.

f) We use this to put food in our mouth.

g) It is made of fruit and we put it on bread.

h) We eat soup or dessert with this.

i) A piece of hot bread.

●○○ 2. Kennst du dich mit britischem Frühstück aus? Welche dieser Lebensmittel sind eher typisch englisch, welche typisch deutsch und welche findet man in beiden Ländern? → Lösung S. 203

bacon • baked beans • bread rolls • cheese • coffee • eggs • ham • honey • jam • marmalade • muesli • sausages • tea • toast • yoghurt

British	German	both

●○○ 3. Wie könntest du eine höfliche Antwort in diesen Situationen geben? Kreuze die beste Antwort an. → Lösung S. 203

a) Your host mother offers you a cup of tea.

- ☐ "Actually, I don't like tea."
- ☐ "I don't normally drink tea. Can I have something else?"
- ☐ "No, thank you."

b) Your host father asks if you would like some more to eat.

- ☐ "No, thank you. It was delicious but I'm full up now!"
- ☐ "No way! That was too much food for me!"
- ☐ "No, I've had enough now."

c) You are about to start a meal with your host family.

Your host mother says "Please start!"

- ☐ "Good appetite!"
- ☐ "Thank you!"
- ☐ "Have a good one!"

●●○ 4. Lies den Dialog zwischen der Austauschschülerin (Theresa) und der Mutter ihrer Gastfamilie (Mrs Dixon). Die Reihenfolge ist allerdings etwas durcheinandergeraten. Bringe den Dialog wieder in die richtige Reihenfolge. → Lösung S. 203

a) *Claire*: OK, if you want something later, just help yourself. So, what do you think of England so far?

b) *Theresa*: Er, I listen to singers like Taylor Swift, or Ed Sheeran.

c) *Claire*: So, Theresa, this is the living room. Come in and sit down.

d) *Theresa*: Well, so far so good! Everyone is really friendly and I think I'm going to enjoy my stay. But I feel a bit nervous about going to school with you next week. I don't know what I can talk about with the other kids in your class.

e) *Claire*: That's great – I like them, too! Hey, listen, I'm meeting up with a few friends this evening for a pizza. Do you want to come?

f) *Theresa*: No, thanks. I'm not thirsty at the moment.

g) *Claire*: Oh, don't worry about that! Just talk about normal stuff. For example, what kind of music do you like?

h) *Theresa*: Oh, yes, I'd love to!

i) *Claire*: You can sit where you want! Would you like something to drink?

j) *Theresa*: Thanks. Shall I sit here on the sofa?

Reihenfolge:

c) _____, _____, _____, _____, _____,

_____, _____, _____, _____, _____

2 Grenzen überqueren: verschiedene Akzente (*Crossing borders: different accents*)

1. Erkennst du Akzente von verschiedenen Teilen Großbritanniens? Höre zu, wie Leute etwas über ihre Heimat sagen und entscheide, wo sie herkommen.

9

→ Lösung S. 203

a) London, England

Speaker ______

b) Glasgow, Scotland

Speaker ______

c) Dublin, Ireland

Speaker ______

d) Liverpool, England

Speaker ______

Scanne den QR-Code und höre den Text an.

3 Ratschläge für eine Reise (*Advice for a trip*)

1. Du bist gerade bei einer Gastfamilie in England. Die Tochter der Familie, Susie, besucht bald deine Familie in Deutschland. Sie hat für den Austausch einen Brief und eine Checkliste bekommen:

→ Lösung S. 204

Dear Exchange Student,
It will soon be time for your trip to Germany! Before you go, have a look at this checklist and make sure you have everything you need for your stay. If you have any questions, call us on 0208 9371 3358 or send us a mail at info@german-exchange.co.uk.
We hope you enjoy your stay in Germany!
Warm regards,
The German Exchange team

CHECKLIST:

ask your host family if you need anything special

- ☐ clothes
- ☐ good walking boots
- ☐ rain jacket
- ☐ shampoo, shower gel, etc.
- ☐ adapter for phone charger
- ☐ books / music
- ☐ passport and visa if you need one
- ☐ euros
- ☐ a present for your host family

●●○ 1. Du rufst mit Susie deine Eltern in Deutschland an, um die Fragen zu klären. Du hilfst Susie und deinen Eltern bei der Verständigung. Versuche jeweils den Inhalt der Sätze in die andere Sprache zu übertragen, so dass Susie sich mit deiner Mutter verständigen kann.

→ Lösung S. 204

Du: Hallo Mama, Susie hat ein paar Fragen an dich. Susie, was möchtest Du sagen?

Susie: I'm really excited about my trip to Germany! I've never been there before!

Du: a) Sie sagt, sie freut sich sehr auf Deutschland. Sie war noch nie da.

Mama: Wir freuen uns auch. Du wirst viel Spaß haben.

Du: b) ______________________________

____

Susie: It says on my list I should ask you about clothes. Do I need lots of warm clothes for my stay?

Du: c) ______________________________

____

Mama: Ja, im Januar ist es sehr kalt hier. Du brauchst eine warme Jacke, Handschuhe und einen Schal.

Du: d) ______________________________

____

____

____

____

Susie: Ah, OK. And what about the walking boots? Do I really need those?

Du: e) ______________________________

Mama: Ja, bring sie bitte mit. Dann können wir in die Berge gehen. Da ist es wirklich schön.

Du: f) ______________________________

____

____

____

Susie: OK, sounds great! Right, another thing on the list is my passport and maybe a visa. But do I need a visa to travel to Germany?

Du: g) ______________________________

____

Mama: Nein, Briten benötigen kein Visum, um nach Deutschland zu fahren.

Du: h) ______________________________

Susie: Good. I'm glad I don't need one. So, I've got one more important question. Would you like to have something special from Britain that I could bring for you?

Du: i) ______________________________

____

____

Mama: Ja, wir lieben englische Schokolade. Das wäre toll!

Du: j) ______________________________

Susie: Great – thanks for the tip!

4 Weltreise: Interkulturelle Begegnungen (*Travelling the world: discovering other cultures*)

●○○ 1. Lies diese Texte über zwei Reisende, die einen Kulturschock hatten, als sie in ein anderes Land gefahren sind.

Anand: spent 4 weeks in Germany

I'm from Delhi in India. When I came to Germany, it was the first time I had been to Europe. I knew that a lot of things would be different, but there were still a lot of surprises! For one thing, people drive carefully here. They stop at red traffic lights and, if you are out walking, you can cross the road safely because there are places for you to cross! Amazing! Another thing is that it is important to be quiet at certain times. In India, there is always noise, at all times of the day and night. But in Germany it is normal to be quiet in the evening, on Sundays, and even around lunch time. If you are noisy at those times, your neighbours will tell you to be quiet!

I quite liked the food I ate with my guest family, although it wasn't spicy so it tasted a bit boring to me! Good bread is very important in Germany. I must say, after a few days, I started to enjoy eating German bread and now I miss it! One more thing I found out is that recycling is very important to Germans. There is one place for paper, one for plastic, and so on. I think this shows that the Germans care about our planet.

Julia: travelled around India for 3 weeks

Of course, I read a lot about India before I went there, but it took me a few days to feel comfortable there. The biggest shock at the beginning of my trip was that there were just so many people, everywhere! You are never alone, and if you take a bus or train, you will get very close to the other passengers, maybe closer than you would like to be! The roads are full of cars and it was really difficult to cross to the other side. If you wait for the cars to stop, you will wait all day! So, you need to learn how to cross the roads like the Indian people: don't be scared, just step onto the road and hope everything will be OK!

Another shock is that there are a lot of poor people on the streets: you see them everywhere. It is not really a nice feeling to see families living on the street. But there isn't much you can do to help. You can give them some money, but that won't really change anything. It is the same with rubbish: there is a lot of it on the streets, but nobody really seems to care. The people I met were very friendly and were happy to help me if I had a problem, for example if I needed to ask the way. And the food is fantastic! Spicy and delicious – I wish I could eat it every day!

●●○ 2. Lies jetzt diese Aussagen und entscheide, ob sie sich auf Anand, Julia oder beide beziehen.

→ Lösung S. 204

a) This person thought the traffic situation was dangerous.

☐ Anand ☐ Julia ☐ both

b) This person felt safer in the country he / she was visiting than at home.

☐ Anand ☐ Julia ☐ both

c) This person was surprised by the way people behaved in the evening.

☐ Anand ☐ Julia ☐ both

d) This person felt bad about a situation he / she saw on his / her trip.

☐ Anand ☐ Julia ☐ both

e) This person found some food that he / she enjoyed eating.

☐ Anand ☐ Julia ☐ both

f) This person talks about a situation that is better than in his / her home country.

☐ Anand ☐ Julia ☐ both

g) This person liked the people he / she met.

☐ Anand ☐ Julia ☐ both

5 Über eine fiktive Reise schreiben (*Imagining a future trip*)

●●○ 1. Du nimmst an einem Gewinnspiel teil, um einen Reisegutschein zu gewinnen. Dazu musst du über eine fiktive Reise schreiben. Stell dir vor, dass du nächstes Jahr eine besondere Reise machst und erzähle von deinem Plan. Schreibe interessant und verwende Verbformen in der Zukunft. Mache dir zuerst ein paar Notizen und dann erstelle deinen Text.

→ Lösung S. 205

Notes:

Where?	
Why?	
When?	
How / travel?	
Who / with?	
What see / do?	

1 Wortschatz: Bei einer Gastfamilie
(Vocabulary: Staying with a host family)

→ Übungen ab S. 193

1. a) bowl b) butter c) tea d) plate e) knife f) fork g) jam h) spoon i) toast
   Lösungswort: breakfast

2.

British	German	both
bacon	bread rolls	coffee
baked beans	cheese	eggs
marmalade	ham	honey
sausages	muesli	jam
	yoghurt	tea
		toast

3. a) "No, thank you." b) "No, thank you. It was delicious but I'm full up now!"
   c) "Thank you!"

4. Reihenfolge: c), j), i), f), a), d), g), b), e), h)

2 Grenzen überqueren: verschiedene Akzente
(*Crossing borders: different accents*)

→ Übungen ab S. 196

1. a) Speaker 3 b) Speaker 4 c) Speaker 2 d) Speaker 1

   Audio script:

   Speaker 1: My city might not be the most beautiful in the world, but it has played an important part in British history! In the past, it was famous for building ships. And it was an important place for travelling by ship: in the 19th century, thousands of people left here to go to America! It is still one of the busiest ports in the country today.
   Another reason people know my city is because of its music scene. One of the most famous bands in the world comes from here, and started their music career here in the 1960s. Do I have to tell you their name? Well, I'll give you a clue: it starts with "B"...

   Speaker 2: I come from a capital city. It isn't in Great Britain, but we all speak English here! My city is on a river called the Liffey, it has lots of old and modern buildings and nice parks, for example St Stephen's Green. Our cathedral is called St Patrick's, and it's named after our country's saint.
   If you want to listen to some traditional music, there are hundreds of places to go all around the city! Listen to musicians playing the violin (or "fiddle", as we like to call it) and singing traditional songs. It won't be long before you start singing, too!

Scanne den QR-Code und höre den Text an.

Speaker 3: I come from the biggest city in the UK, and the best, too, if you ask me! This place has got everything: castles, parks, royal palaces, cathedrals, the parliament, bridges, shops, boat trips ... I could go on and on! There are restaurants with food from every culture in the world, and there are enough theatres, cinemas and museums to make sure you'll never get bored!
A great way to see my city from high up is to take a ride on a big wheel down by the river. On a clear day, you can see all the most important buildings and parks from there.

Speaker 4: The city where I live is not the capital of this country, but it's got the largest population. It wasn't always a popular place to live: in fact, in the past, a lot of people thought it was quite dirty and dangerous. Well, that certainly isn't true now! Today there are lots of reasons to be proud of our city. The old buildings have been renovated, there are lots of new shops and restaurants, and there is a lot of great music and theatre here. And, if you want to get away from the city you only need to travel a short distance to be out in beautiful countryside, with hills and lochs and lots of fresh air!
If you're still not sure what my city is called, I'm sure you can guess from my accent which country it is in ...

3 Ratschläge für eine Reise (*Advice for a trip*)

→ Übungen ab S. 197

1. Musterlösung:

b) My mum says she's looking forward to your visit, too, and you're going to have a lot of fun.
c) Susie will wissen, ob sie warme Kleidung braucht.
d) Yes, it's very cold in January where we live. You need to bring a warm jacket, gloves and a scarf.
e) Susie fragt, ob sie wirklich Wanderschuhe mitbringen soll.
f) Mum says you should bring them, and then we can take a trip to the mountains. It's really beautiful there!
g) Mama, braucht Susie ein Visum für Deutschland?
h) No, British people don't need one.
i) Susie fragt, ob es etwas Besonderes gibt, das sie euch schenken könnte.
j) Mum says she loves English chocolate, so that would be a great present!

4 Weltreise: Interkulturelle Begegnungen (*Travelling the world: discovering other cultures*)

→ Übungen ab S. 200

2. a) Julia b) Anand c) Anand d) Julia e) both f) Anand g) Julia

5 Über eine fiktive Reise schreiben (*Imagining a future trip*)

→ Übungen ab S. 202

1. Musterlösung:

Where?	Australia
Why?	Dream of visiting there
When?	Our winter / their summer
How / travel?	Plane
Who / with?	My sister
What see / do?	Sydney: climb Harbour Bridge; Bondi Beach; visit friends of our parents; swim at Great Barrier Reef

I have big plans for my next holiday. I want to go a very long way from home, and so I've booked a trip to Australia! You might ask yourself why I want to travel so far. Well, it has always been my dream to visit Australia, and so I finally decided to do it. However, I'm not going alone: my sister Michelle is coming with me. It's going to be great!
Well, of course we're travelling by plane: there isn't any other way to get to Australia from here! We are flying from Frankfurt to Sydney, on 14th December. That's right: we're going in winter, but in Australia it will be summer then. My sister and I are really lucky, because we have two months for our trip. That means we will have time to see lots of different things.
We are going to Sydney first because our parents have friends there. We are staying with them for Christmas. I am very excited about having Christmas in a hot country for the first time! My mum's friend, Barbara, said we're going to have a barbeque for Christmas dinner, and then go for a swim at the famous Bondi Beach. While we're in Sydney, I want to see the Opera House and to climb the Harbour Bridge. I think we will be able to get a great view of the city from the top!
But we are not going to stay in Sydney for the whole two months. We are also going to travel north, to the beautiful Great Barrier Reef. We're staying at a hotel on a small island and are going to take a boat trip to the reef every day. It will be amazing to swim with all the colourful fish.
As you can see, it is going to be a very special trip. I am counting the days until 14th December!

Auf dem Land (*In the country*)

1 Die Natur (*The natural world*)

●○○ 1. Sieh das Foto an und fülle die Lücken. → Lösung S. 212

This photo was taken in the countryside, near the a) ______________ . On the right, there is a yellow, sandy b) ______________ . The c) ______________ is clear and blue. There are high brown and green d) ______________ rising up from the beach, with lots of green e) ______________ at the top. It looks like a nice place to go for a walk. On the left-hand side of the picture, there is a high f) ______________ with a road on it. I'm sure there is a beautiful view of the sea from there! In the background, there are some green g) ______________ . I think it would be a nice place to spend a holiday.

●○○ 2. Welches Wort passt nicht zu den anderen? Kreuze an. → Lösung S. 212

a) ☐ woods ☐ forest ☐ cliffs ☐ trees

b) ☐ mountain ☐ lake ☐ valley ☐ hill

c) ☐ field ☐ river ☐ waterfall ☐ lake

d) ☐ grass ☐ flowers ☐ farm ☐ plants

3. Ordne die angegebenen Begriffe in die Tabelle ein → Lösung S. 212

canal • car park • cathedral • church • farmhouse • field • forest • hill • hotel • lake • mountain • museum • park • pond • pub • restaurant • river • school • shop • shopping centre • station • valley • village • waterfall • woods

Town	Countryside	both

4. Ergänze die Sätze mit Wörtern aus der Tabelle. → Lösung S. 212

a) There were lots of horses running in the ________________ .

b) We climbed to the top of the mountain, then walked back down into the ________________ .

c) Freddie grew up in a small ________________ in Wales, but his family moved to Cardiff when he was five.

d) ________________ are very important for our planet. The trees give us clean air and lots of animals live there, too.

e) A ________________ is a nice place to get some fresh air if you live in a city. Lots of trees and flowers grow there, and you can play football on the grass.

f) The bells in the village ________________ started to ring just before midnight on Christmas Eve.

2 Die Tierwelt (*Wildlife*)

●○○ 1. Lies die Beschreibungen und entscheide, um welches Tier es geht.

→ Lösung S. 212

deer • duck • hedgehog • Highland cows • sheep

a) You might find this animal living in your garden. If there are a lot of leaves on the ground, you might hear the animal moving around there. But you won't see it in winter, as it finds somewhere to sleep until the weather gets warm again. If this animal is in danger, it rolls up into a ball so that you can only see the sharp spikes on its back.

____

b) These animals don't care if the weather's cold, because their thick, hairy coats keep them warm. They live in the northern part of Britain, and are a type of animal that gives us milk and meat.

____

c) This animal feels at home in the town or in the country: it just needs a nice lake or pond to live on! It is a type of bird, but one that prefers swimming to flying.

____

d) This animal often lives on a farm. However, you will also find wild ones, in parts of Wales, for example. It's an animal that is useful to people: we make clothes from its wool, and cheese from its milk.

____

e) If you go into the forest, you might see this wild animal. Although it is big, it will not hurt you and might even run away when it sees you. It is easy to see which one is the "man", because he has big horns called antlers on his head!

____

●○○ 2. Lies diese Informationen über Füchse. → Lösung S. 212

What does the fox say?

a) Everybody knows what a fox looks like, even if they have never seen one in real life. People are very interested in foxes, and there are lots of stories about them. Quite often, the fox is the "bad guy", although sometimes, like in Roald Dahl's story "Fantastic Mr Fox", he is the hero. But how much do you really know about foxes? Read our Fun Fox Facts and find out!

b) Foxes are part of the dog family. They look quite like dogs, but have a big, hairy tail. However, in some ways, they are more like cats. When they hunt their food, they watch and follow the animal they want to eat and then jump on it like a cat. Sometimes they do not kill it right away but play with it first – if you have ever seen a cat with a mouse or a bird, you will know what I mean!

c) Foxes are very good hunters. They can see very well, especially at night, but their hearing is also excellent: they can hear quiet sounds from long distances. As well as this, they have special hairs on their faces and legs, which help them find their way. No wonder they can be so dangerous to other small animals!

d) Do you know where foxes live? They normally dig a hole, called a den, and live underground. But sometimes they live above ground, too, in an old tree. They make a comfortable home for themselves and their babies (who are called fox cubs).

e) So why do some people hate foxes and want to hurt them? Well, maybe we can understand that farmers are angry when foxes steal their chickens. But, for a long time, fox hunting was a sport in Britain, which means people killed foxes for fun. Now, however, this is banned and foxes do not have to die in such a horrible way. That's good news!

●●○ 3. Welche Überschrift passt am besten zu den jeweiligen Absätzen? Eine der Überschriften brauchst du nicht. → Lösung S. 212

Paragraph ______ : Fantastic ears and eyes

Paragraph ______ : No more killing

Paragraph ______ : More a dog or a cat?

Paragraph ______ : A fox's favourite food

Paragraph ______ : Good guy or bad guy?

Paragraph ______ : A place to call home

●●○ 4. Kreuze die Aussage an, die am meisten Sinn macht. → Lösung S. 212

a) There are a lot of stories about foxes because

- ☐ writers want to show that they are bad animals.
- ☐ people are interested in reading about them.
- ☐ they are the heroes of the animal world.

b) Foxes are like cats because

- ☐ they are part of the cat family.
- ☐ they like eating birds.
- ☐ they hunt in the same way.

c) At night, foxes

- ☐ can see very well.
- ☐ stay in their den.
- ☐ have to listen very carefully.

d) Farmers often want to kill foxes because

- ☐ they enjoy fox hunting.
- ☐ it is a typical kind of sport in the countryside.
- ☐ foxes kill their animals.

3 Land und Stadt (*Town and country*)

●○○ 1. Du wirst drei Leute hören, die über ihren Wohnort sprechen. Höre genau zu und entscheide, welche Person welche Aussage macht. Bei manchen Aussagen, kannst du mehr als eine Person ankreuzen.

10

→ Lösung S. 213

Speaker 1: Marie

Speaker 2: Patrick

Speaker 3: Jenny

a) She / He has a hobby that would not be possible in a town.

☐ Marie ☐ Patrick ☐ Jenny

b) She / He thinks that the place they live is better for younger children than for older ones.

☐ Marie ☐ Patrick ☐ Jenny

c) She / He likes to be able to do things without her / his parents.

☐ Marie ☐ Patrick ☐ Jenny

d) She / He thinks life is more relaxed in the place where she / he lives.

☐ Marie ☐ Patrick ☐ Jenny

●●○ 2. Höre nochmal zu und verbessere die Aussagen.

→ Lösung S. 213

a) Marie had nowhere to play when she was young.

___

b) Patrick likes to take a break from the internet on holiday.

___

c) Jenny's family moved because the children were unhappy in the city.

___

d) Jenny thinks it will be easy to get a job where she lives now.

___

Scanne den QR-Code und höre den Text an.

1 Auf dem Land (*In the country*)

→ Übungen ab S. 206

1. This photo was taken in the countryside, near the a) **coast**. On the right, there is a yellow, sandy b) **beach**. The c) **sea** is clear and blue. There are high brown and green d) **cliffs** rising up from the beach, with lots of green e) **grass** at the top. It looks like a nice place to go for a walk. On the left-hand side of the picture, there is a high f) **bridge** with a road on it. I'm sure there is a beautiful view of the sea from there! In the background, there are some green g) **hills**. I think it would be a nice place to spend a holiday.

2. a) cliffs b) lake c) field d) farm

3.

Town	Countryside	both
canal	farmhouse	church
car park	field	hill
cathedral	forest	hotel
museum	lake	pond
park	mountain	pub
restaurant	valley	river
shopping centre	village	school
	waterfall	shop
	woods	station

4. a) There were lots of horses running in the **field**. b) We climbed to the top of the mountain, then walked back down into the **valley**. c) Freddie grew up in a small **village** in Wales, but his family moved to Cardiff when he was five. d) **Forests** are very important for our planet. The trees give us clean air and lots of animals live there, too. e) A **park** is a nice place to get some fresh air if you live in a city. Lots of trees and flowers grow there, and you can play football on the grass. f) The bells in the village **church** started to ring just before midnight on Christmas Eve.

2 Die Tierwelt (*Wildlife*)

→ Übungen ab S. 208

1. a) hedgehog b) Highland cows c) duck d) sheep e) deer

3. Paragraph c): Fantastic ears and eyes; Paragraph e): No more killing; Paragraph b): More a dog or a cat?; Paragraph a): Good guy or bad guy?; Paragraph d): A place to call home

4. a) There are a lot of stories about foxes because people are interested in reading about them. b) Foxes are like cats because they hunt in the same way. c) At night, foxes can see very well. d) Farmers often want to kill foxes because foxes kill their animals.

3 Land und Stadt (*Town and country*)

→ Übungen ab S. 211

10

1. Audio script:

Marie: I live in a small village in the middle of the Welsh countryside and I love it here! Well, I did, when I was younger. It's a fantastic place for kids. There are not many cars, so it's very safe, even for young children. Me and my friends always played in the fields and woods, and jumped in the little river in summer to cool off. I love horses and I spend a lot of time helping at a riding school near my house. My parents don't have enough money to give me my own horse, but I can go to the riding school whenever I like. I couldn't do that in a town.

When I was younger, I went to the village school, and so did all of my friends. But there isn't a school for older children here, so we have to go by bus to the nearest town. And now that I go to the town every day, I can see that it is a little bit boring in the village. My friends who live in the town can go shopping for clothes, or go to the cinema, whenever they want to. They can meet up in the afternoons and they don't need to worry about missing the last bus. They have more freedom than the village kids, and I want that now, too.

Patrick: I don't know why anybody would want to live in the countryside! My parents sometimes take us there for a walking holiday and I hate it! Some of the places we stay don't even have wi-fi – what can you do all day if you can't even go online? Just walk around fields looking at horses, or climb hills? What for? I like living in a city. Everything is nearby, and I don't have to ask my parents to drive me everywhere I want to go. I can just take the bus or the train.

Jenny: Last year, I moved to this village with my family. Before that, we lived in London, and my parents wanted to get away from there. At first I didn't like it here at all, but now I do. When we go back to London to visit friends and family, I see how dirty and noisy it is. There is always a lot of traffic and too many people hurrying around. They always seem so busy! Here in the village, people have more time for a chat. And now I really like sitting in the garden in summer, just listening to the sounds of the insects and the animals on the farm down the road.
One problem is, though, that there aren't really any jobs here for young people. It's OK now, but I can see that I will have to move back to the city after I leave school. Most young people here do that.

Scanne den QR-Code und höre den Text an.

a) Marie b) Marie and Jenny c) Patrick d) Jenn

2. a) Marie had lots of places to play, for example in the fields and woods. b) Patrick is unhappy if there is no wi-fi when he is on holiday. c) Jenny's family moved because her parents wanted to leave the city. d) Jenny thinks she will have to move away from the village to get a job.

Musik und Unterhaltung (*Music and entertainment*)

1 Musik (*Music*)

●○○ 1. Finde die passende Vokabel zu diesen Bildern. → Lösung S. 222

a) ______________________________

b) ______________________________

c) ______________________________

d) ______________________________

●○○ 2. Sortiere die Buchstaben der verschiedenen Musikarten. → Lösung S. 222

a) This evening, the London Philharmonic Orchestra will be playing a concert of l s **c** a s i l a c music by Mozart and Beethoven.

b) Winnie is a z **j** a z singer and is performing at Ronnie Scott's night-club tomorrow evening.

c) What kind of music does your band play?" "o k **R** c and o **p** p."

d) o r **W** d l music is a mixture of typical music from different places, for example Africa or South America.

e) In the USA in the 1950s, black people started playing a kind of music called **s** l o u. It comes from gospel and other types of music.

3. Finde zehn Musikinstrumente in dem Wortgitter. → Lösung S. 222

F	L	U	T	E	S	T	X	K
C	G	U	I	T	A	R	V	E
V	B	N	S	P	X	U	I	Y
B	A	S	S	L	O	M	O	B
T	R	U	P	W	P	P	L	O
S	C	P	Q	U	H	E	I	A
P	R	I	D	B	O	T	N	R
C	L	A	R	I	N	E	T	D
Y	D	N	U	W	E	B	T	R
U	I	O	M	O	H	D	F	M

4. Fülle die Lücke mit dem richtigen Verb.
Achte auf die richtige Verbform. → Lösung S. 222

learn • listen to • play • practise • record • rehearse

a) My sister is ____________________ to play the violin. At the moment, the sounds she makes are terrible!

b) We ____________________ for the concert for 2 months so that our performance would be good.

c) If you want to play a musical instrument well, you should ____________________ every day.

d) What kinds of music do you ____________________ ?

e) Ruth can't ____________________ any instruments but she can sing really well.

f) My band has just ____________________ a new song and uploaded it: here's the link.

2 Probleme in der Familie, Kompromisse (*Problems with your family, compromises*)

●○○ 1. Was sind typische Streitpunkte in einer Familie? Ergänze die Sätze mit einem passenden Wort. → Lösung S. 222

fair • loud • messy • share • spend • stay out • turn off

a) Claire's room is very ________________ . She never puts her clothes and books away.

b) I don't like my brother's music and it's much too ________________ ! He should use headphones so I don't have to listen to it.

c) Our house is quite small, so I have to ________________ a bedroom with my sister. I wish I had my own room!

d) You ________________ too much time playing on your phone. You should ______________ it ______________ and do something else!

e) All my friends are allowed to ________________ late at the weekends, but I have to be home by 9.30 p.m. It isn't ________________ !

●●○ 2. Höre jetzt diesen Familien-Streit zu und beantworte die Fragen. → Lösung S. 223

11

a) What does Gracie want Paula to do before her friends come around?

____

b) Where does Paula think Gracie and her friends should go?

____

c) Why does Gracie want to use the room when her friends visit?

____

Scanne den QR-Code und höre den Text an.

d) Why do the two girls have to share a room?

____

e) Why does Gracie think she should be allowed to use the room?

____

f) Do the girls find a compromise?

____

●●○ 12

3. Mum möchte mit Gracie und Paula noch einmal über die Probleme sprechen, damit sie einen Kompromiss finden können. Höre das Gespräch an und ergänze die Sätze.

→ Lösung S. 224

Mum: Ok, you two. a) ________________________ the problems 3with your room without shouting at each other?

Mum: Paula, b) ________________________ about Gracie using the room when her friends are here?

Paula: Well, maybe not. c) ________________________ every weekend!

Gracie: d) ________________________, but we like meeting here.

Paula: e) ________________________, but I don't want to tidy the room just so that you can spend time there with your friends!

Gracie: f) ________________________. I never really thought about it before. OK, g) ________________________ meet at a different friend's house every week.

Paula: OK, h) ________________________ if you only meet here sometimes.

Scanne den QR-Code und höre den Text an.

3 Ein Interview führen (*Interviewing someone*)

1. Du erstellst einen Podcast für eine Webseite zum Thema „Ungewöhnliche Hobbys". Eine Freundin hat ein solches Hobby und du interviewst sie, allerdings auf Englisch, da sie kein Deutsch spricht. Führe das Interview so durch, dass deine deutschen Zuhörer alles verstehen. Denke daran, dass du nicht alles übersetzen musst, sondern den Sinn für deine Zuhörer übertragen sollst.

→ Lösung S. 224

You: Hallo und herzlich willkommen zu der neuesten Ausgabe unseres Schüler-Podcasts! Heute machen wir weiter mit der Serie „Ungewöhnliche Hobbys". Es freut mich sehr, euch meinen heutigen Gast vorzustellen: Joanne Maloney. Sie lebt noch nicht so lange in Deutschland, deshalb werde ich sie auf Englisch befragen.

You: So, hi, Joanne! Danke, dass Du heute hier bist, um mit uns zu sprechen!

Joanne: It's nice to be here! Thanks for inviting me!

You: Ich frage Joanne jetzt, was ihr Hobby ist.

(*Du fragst nach Joannes Hobby.*)

a) ______________________________

Joanne: Well, my hobby is Irish dancing!

(*Du sagst den Zuhörern auf Deutsch, was Joanne gesagt hat.*)

You: b) ______________________________

(*Du fragst Joanne warum sie gerade dieses Hobby hat.*)

You: c) ______________________________

Joanne: Well, as you can see from my name, my dad is Irish, so I'm interested in Irish culture. I have always loved dancing, so it seemed natural to me to learn this special kind of dance.

(*Du erzählst den Zuhörern, worüber ihr gesprochen habt.*)

You: d) ______________________________

____

____

(*Du fragst Joanne was so besonders daran ist.*)

You: e) ______________________________

Joanne: Irish dancing is a bit different to other kinds of dance because you don't really move your arms. Your legs have to do all the work. You have to move your feet very fast and you must be able to jump high, too! If you want to be good at Irish dancing, you have to be very fit!

(*Du erzählst den Zuhörern, worüber ihr gesprochen habt.*)

You: f) ______________________________

____

____

(*Du fragst Joanne, ob es schwierig ist, tanzen zu lernen.*)

You: g) ______________________________

Joanne: It was quite hard at first, yes. As I said, you have to be fit, and you also have to remember a lot of different moves. We often dance in a line, which means you have to do the same moves at the same time as the other dancers.

(*Du erzählst den Zuhörern, worüber ihr gesprochen habt.*)

You: h) ______________________________

____

____

(*Du fragst Joanne, ob man besondere Kleidung benötigt.*)

You: i) ______________________________

Joanne: Yes, we wear special clothes when we dance. The girls wear beautiful, colourful dresses. The dresses are quite short, so you can see our legs moving. We wear special shoes, too, that make quite a loud noise as we jump around!

(*Du erzählst den Zuhörern, worüber ihr gesprochen habt.*)

You: j) ______________________________

____

____

(*Du fragst Joanne, wo man tanzt.*)

You: k) ______________________________

Joanne: You can see Irish dancing at ceilidhs, for example, or at weddings and parties. There are also a lot of dance competitions, but I am not good enough to take part in those.

(*Du erzählst den Zuhörern, worüber ihr gesprochen habt.*)

You: l) ______________________________

____

____

(*Du bedankst dich für das Interview.*)

You: m) ______________________________

Joanne: No problem! It was nice talking to you!

1 Musik (*Music*)

→ Übungen ab S. 215

1. a) orchestra b) choir c) band d) singer

2. a) This evening, the London Philharmonic Orchestra will be playing a concert of **classical** music by Mozart and Beethoven. b) Winnie is a **jazz** singer and is performing at Ronnie Scott's nightclub tomorrow evening. c) "What kind of music does your band play?" "**Rock** and **pop**." d) **World** music is a mixture of typical music from different places, for example Africa or South America. e) In the USA in the 1950s, black people started playing a kind of music called **soul**. It comes from gospel and other types of music.

3.

F	**L**	**U**	**T**	**E**	**S**	**T**	X	**K**
C	**G**	**U**	**I**	**T**	**A**	**R**	**V**	**E**
V	B	N	S	P	**X**	**U**	**I**	**Y**
B	**A**	**S**	**S**	L	**O**	**M**	**O**	**B**
T	R	U	P	W	**P**	**P**	**L**	**O**
S	C	**P**	Q	U	**H**	**E**	**I**	**A**
P	R	**I**	**D**	B	**O**	**T**	**N**	**R**
C	**L**	**A**	**R**	**I**	**N**	**E**	**T**	**D**
Y	D	**N**	**U**	W	**E**	B	T	R
U	I	**O**	**M**	O	H	D	F	M

flute, guitar, bass, clarinet, piano, drum, saxophone, trumpet, violin, keyboard

4. a) My sister is **learning** to play the violin. At the moment, the sounds she makes are terrible! b) We **rehearsed** for the concert for 2 months so that our performance would be good. c) If you want to play a musical instrument well, you should **practise** every day. d) What kinds of music do you **listen to**? e) Ruth can't **play** any instruments but she can sing really well. f) My band has just **recorded** a new song and uploaded it: here's the link.

2 Probleme in der Familie, Kompromisse (*Problems with your family, compromises*)

→ Übungen ab S. 217

1. a) Claire's room is very **messy**. She never puts her clothes and books away. b) I don't like my brother's music and it's much too **loud**! He should use headphones so I don't have to listen to it. c) Our house is quite small, so I have to **share** a bedroom with my sister. I wish I had my own room! d) You **spend** too much time playing on your phone. You should **turn** it **off** and do something else! e) All my friends are allowed to **stay out** late at the weekends, but I have to be home by 9.30 p.m. It isn't **fair**!

2. Audio script:

Mum: Gracie! Paula! Stop shouting at each other! What are you fighting about now? Come down here and talk to me!
Gracie: Oh, I am so sick of sharing this room with my stupid sister!
Paula: You're stupid, not me!
Gracie: Oh, shut up!
Paula: You shut up!
Mum: Girls, stop it now! Why don't you stop shouting and talk about the problem? What's wrong, Gracie?
Gracie: Well, you know my friends are coming around later. And Paula's side of the room is so messy! I don't want to sit with my friends looking at all her clothes and make-up. She should tidy up her things before they come.
Paula: Why should I? It's my room, too. You always send me out when your friends come, but I can stay in the room if I want to. Why don't you all go and sit in the living room?
Gracie: Because we want to talk about personal things, that's why!
Paula: Oooh, want to talk about your boyfriends, do you?
Gracie: It's none of your business what we talk about! Why do we still have to share a room, anyway? It isn't fair!
Mum: Now don't be silly, Gracie. You know you can't both have your own room. I have to use the other bedroom as an office when I work from home. Let's see if we can find a compromise.
Gracie: I don't want a compromise! I'm the oldest, so I should be allowed to use the room to meet my friends whenever I want to! So, Paula has to tidy up and then get out! There's nothing else to talk about! (sound of door slamming shut)
Paula: See, Mum – you can't even talk to her. Well, I'm not going to tidy up anything! If she wants to use the room, she can tidy it herself.
Mum: Girls, really …

a) Gracie wants Paula to tidy up her side of their room. b) Paula thinks Gracie and her friends should go to the living room. c) Gracie and her friends want to talk about personal things. d) They have to share because their mother works in the other bedroom. e) Gracie thinks she should be allowed to use the room because she is older than Paula. f) No, they don't.

Scanne den QR-Code und höre den Text an.

12

3. Audio script:

Mum: OK, you two. Can we talk about the problems with your room without shouting at each other?

Gracie: OK, fine. Let's talk.

Mum: Paula, how do you feel about Gracie using the room when her friends are here? Is it really so unfair?

Paula: Well, maybe not. But her friends come here every weekend! Why can't they go somewhere else?

Gracie: You've got a point, but we like meeting here. And it would be perfect if the room was tidy!

Paula: That's true, but I don't want to tidy the room just so that you can spend time there with your friends! Just because you're older than me, you think I always have to do what you want!

Gracie: Hmm, I guess you're right. I never really thought about it before. OK, I've got an idea. Maybe we could meet at a different friend's house every week. Then we would only be here sometimes. But you have to tidy your side of the room before they come and then leave us alone for the afternoon. What do you think about that?

Paula: OK, I don't mind if you only meet here sometimes. And I'll try not to be so messy!

Gracie: Thanks!

Ok, you two. a) **Can we talk about** the problems with your room without shouting at each other? Paula, b) **how do you feel** about Gracie using the room when her friends are here? Well, maybe not. c) **But her friends come here** every weekend! d) You've got a point, but we like meeting here. e) **That's true**, but I don't want to tidy the room just so that you can spend time there with your friends! f) **I guess you're right**. I never really thought about it before. OK, g) **I've got an idea. Maybe we could** meet at a different friend's house every week. OK, h) **I don't mind** if you only meet here sometimes.

Scanne den QR-Code
und höre den Text an.

3 Ein Interview führen (*Interviewing someone*)

→ Übungen ab S. 219

1. Musterlösung:

a) So, Joanne, what's your hobby?
b) Joanne sagt, ihr Hobby ist Irish dancing.
c) And why did you start doing/why are you interested in Irish dancing?
d) Ich habe gefragt, warum gerade Irish dancing und Joanne erzählt, dass ihr Vater aus Irland kommt und sie deshalb an Irischer Kultur interessiert ist. Und nachdem sie Tanzen immer geliebt hat, war es für sie ganz normal, diese Tanz-Art zu lernen.
e) So what's special about Irish dancing?
f) Meine Frage war, was besonders ist an Irish dancing und Joanne meint, dass der Unterschied zu anderen Tanz-Arten ist, dass man dabei die Arme nicht viel bewegt. Die Bewegung kommt von den Beinen. Man muss die Füße sehr schnell bewegen und hoch springen können. Irische Tänzer müssen fit sein.
g) Is Irish dancing difficult to learn? / Is it difficult to learn Irish dancing?
h) Ich wollte von Joanne wissen, ob es schwierig ist, das zu lernen. Sie erzählt, dass Irish dancing schon relative schwierig zu lernen war, weil man sich viele Schritte merken muss. Es wird oft in einer Reihe getanzt, und alle Tänzer müssen sich gleichzeitig bewegen.
i) And do you wear special clothes when you dance?
j) Ich habe gefragt, was man zum Tanzen anziehen muss. Joanne sagt, dass die Mädchen schöne bunte Kleider tragen, die relativ kurz sind. Damit kann man die Bein-Bewegungen besser sehen. Sie tragen auch besondere Schuhe, die viel Krach machen!
k) And where can you see Irish dancing?
l) Ich wollte wissen, wo man Irish dancing erleben kann. Joanne sagt, man sieht es bei Ceilidhs, oder auf Hochzeiten und Partys. Es gibt auch Wettbewerbe, aber da nimmt Joanne nicht teil.
m) Joanne, thank you very much for this interview!

Das Leben als Teenager (*Teenage life*)

1 Gefühle ausdrücken (*Talking about your feelings*)

●○○ 1. Ergänze die Sätze mit dem richtigen Wort, um auszudrücken, wie die Personen sich fühlen.

→ Lösung S. 234

angry • disappointed • nervous • scared • shy • upset

a) Tom doesn't talk very much when he meets new people because he's quite ____________________ .

b) Will your parents be ____________________ when they find out about the party?

c) I'm quite ____________________ about the maths test. I wish I had worked harder.

d) Lisa was ____________________ when she didn't get the job she wanted.

e) We felt quite ____________________ when we spent the night alone in that big old house. I think we had watched too many horror films!

f) Ben has got a new girlfriend. His old girlfriend, Poppy, is very ____________________ about it.

●○○ 2. Wie fühlt man sich in diesen Situationen? Wähle das richtige Wort.

→ Lösung S. 234

a) I feel angry / guilty / sad because I lied to my mum about where I was going last weekend.

b) She was happy / confused / afraid when she won the competition.

c) We were nervous / shocked / disappointed when we heard about the accident.

d) I am afraid / guilty / worried about the test. I hope I got a good mark!

e) It's my birthday today! Of course I feel shy / fantastic / sad!

●○○ 3. Wie beschreibt man am besten, wie man sich in solchen Situationen fühlt? Wähle ein passendes Wort. → Lösung S. 234

a) You are talking to your boyfriend / girlfriend on the phone and are saying some quite personal things. When you have finished talking, you find out that your dad was listening to you.

b) You worked very hard on your school project, spent a lot of time finding information on the internet and printed out lots of pictures to really make it look good. But your teacher did not really like it and only gave you a "C".

c) You and a friend have been asked to give a talk to the whole school about a project that your class has been working on. On the day of the talk, your friend is ill and you have to give the talk by yourself.

scary — nervous — guilty — confused — disappointed — embarrassed

●○○ 4. Was antwortest du auf die angegebene Aussage? → Lösung S. 234

a) "Oh, sorry – I've broken a plate."

b) "I apologize for being so late."

c) "You really hurt my feelings when you said my new haircut looked stupid."

"Never mind. You're here now."

"OK, but be more careful next time!"

"I'm sorry. I didn't mean to be rude."

"Well, don't do it again!"

"You're always late! I don't know why we wait for you."

2 Umzug in ein anderes Land (*Moving to a different country*)

●○○ 1. Lies den Dialog zwischen Lucy und ihren Eltern. → Lösung S. 234

Lucy's father is a teacher. He is taking part in a programme in which he can exchange jobs with another teacher in a different part of the world. He has just heard that he has got a job in Mexico.

Dad: Come and sit down, everybody! I've got something to tell you.

Mum: Lucy, take your headphones off and listen! This is important!

Dad: OK, here comes the big news ... We're going to Mexico!

Lucy: Mexico? Why Mexico? That's so far away!

Dad: Well, that's the job I've been offered. And, if you remembered, we talked about going somewhere completely different, so that it's more of an adventure.

Lucy: Humph, that was your idea! I don't want to go anywhere at all!

Mum: Come on, Lucy. We've talked about this a lot. And we all agreed that we would like to live somewhere different for a while. You agreed, too! It isn't forever, just for a couple of years.

Lucy: A couple of years! How can we live in Mexico for a couple of years? We don't even speak Spanish!

Mum: Well, remember, that's one reason we want to go, to learn another language. Don't worry - you'll learn it very quickly when we're there! And you're going to go to the International School, so everyone will speak English there. I'm sure you'll soon make new friends.

Lucy: But what if I don't? And maybe I don't want to make new friends! I want to stay here with my old friends. I'll miss out on so much if I don't see them every day.

Dad: Well, maybe you won't see them every day, but you can still chat to them online. And don't forget that you can do video chats, too.

Lucy: But the time zones are so different! When I have time to chat, my friends will be in bed!

Mum: Well, some of your friends seem to be online day and night, so I'm sure that won't be a problem. And you can have a video chat at the weekend.

Lucy: OK, there's something I haven't told you yet. There's a reason I don't want to move away any more. I, well, I met this boy at Jackie's party two weeks ago, and he's really great! If we go away, he'll split up with me.

Dad: Well, that's certainly not a reason to change our plans! You're too young for a serious boyfriend anyway.

Lucy: You don't understand! I hate you! I'm going out!
(*leaves the room*)

●○○ 2. Kreuze jetzt die beste Antwort an. → Lösung S. 234

a) Lucy's parents want to go to Mexico because
- ☐ it is a good way of learning Spanish.
- ☐ they don't like living in Europe.
- ☐ they want the chance to live somewhere with a different culture.

b) Lucy
- ☐ never wanted to move away.
- ☐ agreed to go but has now changed her mind.
- ☐ wants to go to a country where she can speak the language.

c) When they are in Mexico
- ☐ Lucy will meet other kids who speak English.
- ☐ the family will need a lot of Spanish lessons.
- ☐ it will be difficult to learn a new language.

d) Lucy doesn't want to leave her old friends because
- ☐ they won't talk to her any more if she goes.
- ☐ she won't know what is happening in their lives if she doesn't see them often.
- ☐ she finds it difficult to make new friends.

e) She thinks it will be hard to keep in touch with her old friends because
- ☐ Mexico is in a different time zone.
- ☐ her friends are not allowed to chat online at the weekend.
- ☐ they have to go to bed earlier than she does.

f) The real reason Lucy doesn't want to move is
- ☐ it will be too difficult to chat with her friends at the weekend.
- ☐ she is in love with a boy.
- ☐ her friends will miss her.

●○○ 3. Lies jetzt den zweiten Text und entscheide, ob die Aussagen richtig oder falsch sind.

→ Lösung S. 234

Later that day, Lucy goes online to chat with her best friend, Katie.

Katie: Hey, Luce. What's going on? You sound terrible.

Lucy: Oh, my dad's got a job in a school in Mexico, and we're leaving in a few weeks!

Katie: Wow. But that's really exciting, isn't it?

Lucy: What do you mean? Are you happy that I'm leaving or something? Won't you miss me?

Katie: Yes, of course I will, but we'll still be able to chat a lot. I'll tell you something: I'd go if I had the chance! I hate our school and all the stupid teachers. And girls in our class get on my nerves! I'd love a break from all of that.

Lucy: Well, I know what you mean, but I still don't want to change schools right now. What if I don't like the kids at my new school? And I've got to tell you something else. You know Rob Cramer? Well, we, er, kissed at Jackie's party, and now he keeps messaging me. I really don't want to go away right now.

Katie: Rob Cramer? Stay away from him – he's bad news! You know he's got a girlfriend, right? But he's always messaging other girls.

Lucy: What?! Well, if that's true, I'm glad I'm leaving …

	true	false
a) Katie is happy that Lucy is going away.	☐	☐
b) Lucy is excited about moving.	☐	☐
c) The girls will have a lot of contact while Lucy is away.	☐	☐
d) Lucy doesn't know if she will make new friends.	☐	☐
e) Rob Cramer has split up with his girlfriend.	☐	☐

3 Etwas aus einer anderen Perspektive erzählen (*Telling a story from a different point of view*)

1. Lies diesen Auszug aus einer Geschichte. → Lösung S. 234

Paul left school later than the others that day. Before he left the building, he went to the library to get a book for his homework. Or that's what he told himself. But he knew what was really going on. He was wasting time, doing everything more slowly, because he hoped that Craig and the others would not wait for him. If he took a long time, they would get bored and go home, or at least go and find somebody else to bully.

After half an hour, he thought he might be safe. He walked slowly to the school gates and looked carefully down the street. There was nobody there. Paul felt happier than he had felt all day. It was as if he had been carrying something heavy on his back, and suddenly it was gone.

He lived quite near the school, and on the way home he thought about what he would do when he got there. Make himself a sandwich, have something to drink. Surf the internet for a while before he started his homework. Forget about Craig and his mates, at least until the next morning. But when he turned the corner to his road, he got a bad shock, because there was somebody sitting on his parents' garden wall. It was Craig.

2. Erzähle jetzt dieselbe Geschichte aus der Ich-Perspektive. Überlege zuerst, was die Unterschiede zu einer Erzählung in der dritten Person sind. In der ersten Person erleben die Leser die Geschichte mit dir und sehen die Ereignisse mit deinen Augen. Du kannst als Erzähler deine Gefühle zeigen und Spannung in die Geschichte bringen. → Lösung S. 234

1 Gefühle ausdrücken (*Talking about your feelings*)

→ Übungen ab S. 226

1. a) Tom doesn't talk very much when he meets new people because he's quite **shy**. b) Will your parents be **angry** when they find out about the party? c) I'm quite **nervous** about the math's test. I wish I had worked harder. d) Lisa was **disappointed** when she didn't get the job she wanted. e) We felt quite **scared** when we spent the night alone in that big, old house. I think we had watched too many horror films! f) Ben has got a new girlfriend. His old girlfriend, Poppy, is very **upset** about it.

2. a) I feel **guilty** because I lied to my mum about where I was going last weekend. b) She was **happy** when she won the competition. c) We were **shocked** when we heard about the accident. d) I am **worried** about the test. I hope I got a good mark! e) It's my birthday today! Of course I feel **fantastic**!

3. a) embarrassed b) disappointed c) nervous

4. a) "OK, but be more careful next time!" b) "Never mind. You're here now." c) "I'm sorry. I didn't mean to be rude."

2 Umzug in ein anderes Land (*Moving to another country*)

→ Übungen ab S. 228

2. a) Lucy's parents want to go to Mexico because they want the chance to live somewhere with a different culture. b) Lucy agreed to go but has now changed her mind. c) When they are in Mexico Lucy will meet other kids who speak English. d) Lucy doesn't want to leave her old friends because she won't know what is happening in their lives if she doesn't see them often. e) She thinks it will be hard to keep in touch with her old friends because Mexico is in a different time zone. f) The real reason Lucy doesn't want to move is she is in love with a boy.

3. a) false b) false c) true d) true e) false

3 Etwas aus einer anderen Perspektive erzählen (*Telling a story from a different point of view*)

→ Übungen ab S. 232

1. Musterlösung:

   That day, I waited at school until everyone else had gone home. I pretended I needed an extra book to do my homework, so I went to the library at the end of the last lesson. Of course, I didn't really need it, but I spent a long time in the library, looking at all the different books about Roman Britain, until Mrs Hart told me to go home. I hoped I had been slow enough, and that Craig and his gang were not waiting for me. One good thing about those idiots was that they got bored quickly. Maybe they had even found somebody else to bully. That would give me a break!

After half an hour, I thought it was safe to leave. I didn't hurry to the gates, and, before I went through them, I looked up and down the street. Empty. Suddenly, I felt fantastic, almost as if I could dance down the street. I didn't, of course. I don't want to give people even more reasons to think I'm crazy.

While I was walking home, I was thinking about what I would do for the rest of the afternoon. I was hungry, so I decided to make myself a sandwich and have a drink. There was some history homework to do, of course, but that could wait. First I wanted to check out a new game website I had read about. Anything to forget about that idiot Craig. Stop! Don't think about him. Worry about him tomorrow.

I turned the corner and stopped dead. I couldn't believe my eyes. Craig was sitting on our garden wall!

Infinitive	Simple Past	Past Participle	German
be	was/were	been	sein
become	became	become	werden
begin	began	begun	beginnen, anfangen
break	broke	broken	zerbrechen, kaputtgehen
bring	brought	brought	bringen
build	built	built	bauen
buy	bought	bought	kaufen
cut	cut	cut	schneiden
do	did	done	tun, machen
drink	drank	drunk	trinken
drive	drove	driven	ein Fahrzeug führen (Auto/Bus)
eat	ate	eaten	essen
fall	fell	fallen	(hin)fallen
feel	felt	felt	fühlen, sich fühlen
fight	fought	fought	kämpfen
find	found	found	finden
fly	flew	flown	fliegen
forget	forgot	forgotten	vergessen
get	got	got, gotten	bekommen, kriegen, holen, besorgen
give	gave	given	geben
go	went	gone	gehen
grow	grew	grown	wachsen
have	had	had	haben

Infinitive	Simple Past	Past Participle	German
hear	heard	heard	hören
hide	hid	hidden	verstecken
hit	hit	hit	schlagen
hold	held	held	halten
keep	kept	kept	(be)halten
know	knew	known	wissen, kennen
lay	laid	laid	legen
learn	learned	learned	lernen
leave	left	left	verlassen, weg-gehen, abfahren
lie	lay	lain	liegen
lose	lost	lost	verlieren
make	made	made	machen
mean	meant	meant	bedeuten
meet	met	met	(sich) treffen
pay	paid	paid	bezahlen
put	put	put	legen, stellen
read	read	read	lesen
ride	rode	ridden	reiten, Rad fahren
ring	rang	rung	klingeln
run	ran	run	rennen, laufen
say	said	said	sagen
see	saw	seen	sehen
sell	sold	sold	verkaufen
send	sent	sent	schicken, senden

Infinitive	Simple Past	Past Participle	German
set	set	set	setzen, stellen, legen
shine	shone	shone	scheinen
show	showed	shown	zeigen
sing	sang	sung	singen
sit	sat	sat	sitzen, sich setzen
sleep	slept	slept	schlafen
speak	spoke	spoken	sprechen
stand	stood	stood	stehen, sich hinstellen
swim	swam	swum	schwimmen
take	took	taken	nehmen
teach	taught	taught	lehren, unterrichten
tell	told	told	erzählen, berichten
think	thought	thought	denken
throw	threw	thrown	werfen
understand	understood	understood	verstehen
wear	wore	worn	anhaben, tragen (Kleidung)
win	won	won	gewinnen
write	wrote	written	schreiben

Bildquellenverzeichnis

Fotolia New York: 165.6 (Erica Guilane-Nachez), 196.4 (Pefkos), 196.3 (spanishjohnny72), 196.1 (Iakov Kalinin), 196.2 (photoenthusiast); **iStockphoto Calgary, Alberta:** 156, 160 (Pingebat); **Pohle, Marlene Stuttgart:** 155; **Shutterstock New York:** 30.4 (DGLimages), 33.1 (Mike Charles), 33.2 (Edwin Verin), 33.3 (Katherine Welles), 50.1 (matimix), 50.2 (Suzanne Tucker), 135.4 (Lance Bellers), 165.5 (Debu55y), 187 (zhu difeng), 221 (Kobby Dagan), 232 (Tomas Urbelionis); **Thinkstock München:** 30.1 (walterbilotta), 30.2 (Wavebreakmedia), 50.3 (Peter Sterling), 50.4 (Dirima), 53.1 (martinturzak), 53.2 (Marjan_Apostolovic), 53.3 (luckyraccoon), 53.4 (ZbigniewWantuch), 64 (JackF), 77 (Creatas Images), 79.1 (Ron Chapple Stock), 79.2 (BrianAJackson), 79.3 (GlobalP), 79.4 (BananaStock), 86.1 (scanrail), 86.2 (igabriela), 86.4 (Hemera Technologies), 86.5 (LeventKonuk), 100.1 (victorass88), 100.2 (SVproduction), 100.3 (STUDIOGRANDOUEST), 100.3 (ulkas), 100.5 (Anton_Sokolov), 100.6 (seread), 107.1 (eranicle), 107.2 (Rohappy), 107.3 (Purestock), 107.4 (Monkey Business Images), 112 (Fly_Fast), 135.1 (PetersenN), 135.2 (Jupiterimages), 152 (godrick), 161.1 (mauinow1), 161.2 (ritchiedigital), 161.3 (Vectorchoice), 161.4 (miroslav_1), 163 (PeterHermesFurian), 165.1 (TonyBaggett), 165.2 (nazlisart), 165.3 (GeorgiosArt), 165.4 (JustinBlackStock), 173 (filrom), 180 (tuulijumala), 183 (Pavel Losevsky), 185 (shironosov), 189 (Jupiterimages), 198 (Jochen Sand), 199 (Bluberries), 206 (Laura Ciapponi / Design Pics), 209 (jimfeng), 215.1 (cyano66), 215.2 (Highwaystarz-Photography), 215.3 (Jupiterimages), 215.4 (Digital Vision), 217 (Goldfaery), 229 (Buccina Studios)

Passend zum Schulbuch üben!

ISBN: 978-3-12-562526-6

Passend für:
Cornelsen À plus! 1 (Ausgabe 2004)
Cornelsen À plus! 1 Nouvelle édition
Klett Découvertes 1 (Ausgabe 2004)
Klett Découvertes 1 Série jaune
Klett Découvertes 1 Série bleue

ISBN: 978-3-12-562522-8

Passend für:
Diesterweg Camden Town 1
Cornelsen English G 21 A1
Cornelsen English G access 1
Klett Green Line 1 (Ausgabe 2006)
Klett Green Line 1 (Ausgabe 2014)

ISBN: 978-3-12-562523-5

Passend für:
Diesterweg Camden Town 2
Cornelsen English G 21 A2
Cornelsen English G access 2
Klett Green Line 2 (Ausgabe 2006)
Klett Green Line 2 (Ausgabe 2015)

ISBN: 978-3-12-562527-3

Passend für:
Cornelsen À plus! 2 (Ausgabe 2004)
Cornelsen À plus! 2 Nouvelle édition
Klett Découvertes 2 (Ausgabe 2004)
Klett Découvertes 2 Série jaune
Klett Découvertes 2 Série bleue

- Wegweiser passend zu deinem Schulbuch
- Übungen zu Grammatik, Schreiben von eigenen Texten, Leseverstehen, Sprachmittlung
- Alle Übungen mit ausführlichen Lösungen
- QR-Codes zum Download von Hörverstehensübungen

PONS

www.pons.de